ROAST LAMB IN THE OLIVE GROVES

ROAST LAMB IN THE OLIVE GROVES

A MEDITERRANEAN COOKBOOK

Belinda Harley

Photography by Jonathan Lovekin

hardie grant books
MELBOURNE · LONDON

CONTENTS

INTRODUCTION

It is Easter Sunday morning. Across the island, church bells are ringing and so many families are outside in the bright sunshine, their children watching intently as the Easter lamb is turned on a spit, so that as you walk along the old stone donkey paths that lead from village to village, the scent of roast lamb wafts to you through the olive groves …

If you look on a small-scale map of the Ionian sea, the little island of Paxos and its even tinier sibling, Antipaxos, are sometimes omitted entirely. It is as if they have simply been left to the imagination ...

It could be said that the Paxiots have been blessed, even by their misfortunes Scattered in the sea below the heel of Italy, they were at a strategic point in the Mediterranean, like their bigger neighbour Corfu. They were prey to serial occupation down the centuries, as invaders took possession and were ousted in turn. But they came bearing gifts: the Romans built magnificent *sterna*, cisterns to collect water; the Venetians spent four centuries bribing the locals to plant thousands of olive trees. These changed the island's landscape entirely, and yield some of the best, grass-green olive oil in the world.

History is alive in the kitchen. Venetians brought risotto, pasta and an Italian sense of style; the hated Turks awakened the Paxiots' palates to spices; Napoleon's favourite béchamel – *besamel* to the Paxiots – adorns today's *moussaka*. And when Paxiots have had a hard night of celebration, they clear their heads with *tzintzibira*, English ginger beer, from a recipe left behind by the Victorians. The Paxiots adopted the things they liked and infused them, like powerful aromatics, into basic Greek cooking. Recently, they have been showing an unexpected interest in curries...

This is not a traditional Greek cookbook. I am not Greek and one would need the knowledge handed down over centuries, through families, that is the hallmark and inheritance of a native Greek cook. I hope this book does something different: it records the ancient ways; it shows you how to cook in their style, and be inspired by their natural ingredients to make culinary voyages of your own.

I owe this book to Spiros Taxidi, who showed me the food of the island: he is both a mentor and a brother. He and his fellow Paxiots show how it is possible to live simply, and gloriously, on what grows each season. They remind us of something that, deep down, we always knew: that food is better, when it is truthful.

Our word 'diet' comes from the ancient Greek word *dieta*. It means *way of life*: and this is a way of life based on fruit, vegetables, natural grains and pulses full of fibre; freshly made cheeses and yoghurts; fish, poultry and occasionally a little red meat. It is a 'peasant diet' in that it is just the sort of Mediterranean diet that nutritionists now recognise as one of the healthiest.

Food here is a way of life and the local people still follow the old ways. They cook ancient recipes: simple dishes handed down the generations, until they become instinctive – in which good ingredients are allowed to speak for themselves.

On Paxos, cooks still rely, just as they did in ancient times, on the natural flavour of what they grow. They prefer extra-virgin olive oil that has been cold-pressed, rather than industrially produced. They make cheeses from the milk of their own sheep and goats. They are proud of their foraging skills underwater, in collecting shellfish and in fishing. Meat and poultry comes from animals that are grazed on hillsides that have never known pesticides. These Paxiots use herbs and spices astutely in their dishes, with an intuitive, exquisite judgement.

Finally, the reason this food is so glorious is something to do with the Paxiots themselves. They enter into the spirit of religious festivals, saints' days, weddings and family occasions with a seriousness of community purpose – and childlike joy.

They believe that life is to be celebrated: and it should be celebrated with food.

MY FIRST TASTE

Many years ago, a fisherman on Corfu with a battered wooden caique agreed to take us to see the nearby island of Paxos; he said it would take five or six hours to get there. At noon, the heat became brutal. The sea was glassy and eerily flat. Suddenly we heard a cacophony, as of knives and forks beating on a drum: like tinnitus, it was coming from the island. Cicadas. The whole of Paxos was throbbing with them.

Otherwise, the island seemed to be dead to the world. We landed at a tiny fishing village, where the lanes were no more than narrow footpaths between closed, shuttered buildings. Even the cats had hidden from the heat, curled up deftly in the shade. Our Corfiot fisherman banged a closed front door. 'My cousin,' he explained. A generous moustache and a stubbled chin appeared at the door. Then another cousin. Then another. Rough slapping of hands, proffering of cigarettes, rousing the women of the house. We were too many for the tiny kitchen, so the family table and chairs were simply moved outside to receive us: the dining room had become an informal street taverna.

'It is only vegetables,' said the fisherman apologetically, aware that tourists expected meat. Oh, those vegetables … great glistening discs of tomato, with flakes of salt and basil; pale jade hearts of artichoke; woody, dark green spinach; rustic bread, with salty-sweet black olives; and a plate of cool *tzatziki*, which hummed with garlic. I have never forgotten the taste.

Riding pillion on the cousins' Vespas, we bumped over tracks through the olive groves to an even smaller fishing village: Loggos. There was no-one about. A small white jetty stretched like a finger into the sea. We dived into cold turquoise water, then lay like lizards on the rocks to dry our bodies. At that far-off time, I had no idea how often I would return to that jetty, to moor a small boat and watch the world go by; to sit on the 'nosey bench' with the old ladies who sat exchanging the village news …

So like the *helidonia*, the swallows, who make a journey of thousands of miles from Africa to build their nests on the sheer Eremitis cliffs, swooping and diving in acrobatics of exhilaration overhead, I too became a migrant. And each time I returned, I appreciated the food of Paxos and its deceptive simplicity, more. When offered a Michelin-starred menu in London, why did I feel a pang of disappointment, like a child given expensive Christmas presents who suddenly cries out for a much-loved familiar toy? The words '*fine dining*' suddenly sounded artificial, wrong; I wanted *food*.

I am conscious of irony in writing this book in celebration of the Greek way of life, at a time when the Greek people are in trouble. The financial situation has dragged the country into a vortex of poverty; its people, burdened by national debt, leeched by corruption, are near despair.

Yet somehow it is all the more relevant. Through all this darkness, the national spirit is perhaps even more brightly lit; the pride, more bullish; and the food – the simple, honest food that is such a mirror of Greekness – is the more valued. The old ways are remembered all too vividly by those now standing in line at soup kitchens on the streets of Athens for a plate of the same bean stew that would once have been the daily diet on which their ancestors survived. For once the politicians, the economists and the pundits cannot predict what will happen; my own guess is that, although scarred by its losses, with profound regret and dismay, and an eloquent, world-weary shrug, Greece will do what it does best: muddle through.

THE KNOWLEDGE

Two small girls were sitting on top of a rough stone wall beside an almond tree, intent on something important. Each had made a bowl in the lap of her skirt, into which she had collected a mound of fresh almonds – still in their thick green pods, covered with that fine white which feels like suede. Expert teeth and tongues delved for the sweetness of the kernel. When they heard me coming, they raised grave, shy eyes and smiled uncertainly. I greeted them in Greek; but they had already returned to their almonds.

Why, I thought, don't I know what to do with almonds straight from the tree?

Blinded by convenience products in supermarkets, many of us have forgotten what once we knew about food. We have lost precious knowledge – knowledge that was born out of the need to make the very best of what little you have. Growing and tending your own, you value your vegetables for their taste, rather than their looks; you learn to use every scrap of meat from an animal you have reared yourself. Much of this knowledge still survives on the island; although, at a time of acute financial pressure, the old ways are under threat.

Of course, not all food on the island is exemplary, or even good. In summer, when the island throbs with cars and crowds, the tavernas reflect the tourists' tastes, full English breakfasts appear on menus – and pressure of numbers wanting to dine sometimes overpowers quality in the hard-pressed kitchen. The locals, working till late and rising at dawn, have little time to cook for themselves. So you are likely to find Paxiot home cooking at its best out of season.

Spiro: a walking, singing, foraging, cooking guardian of the island's heritage. I would often see him arriving mid-morning on a battered Vespa hand-painted the colour of red wine, with dark circles under his eyes from a string of late nights. Long, black corkscrew curls like those on a Byzantine icon were tied behind his neck to reveal a face that radiated intelligence and wry amusement. He was patron of the *Taxidi*, a bar which he had converted from an old customs house at the end of the white jetty stretching into the sea. Drink in hand, you could look into the tiny harbour on one side, or scan the channel for elusive glimpses of dolphins on the other.

From tiny wild herbs to folklore, from architecture to cooking, he studied and preserved with passion. He knew where to find wild arum lilies in the hills; he mended fishermen's giant panniers and filled them with watermelons to make cocktails with iced vodka. At the bar he would prepare wafer-thin slices of freshly-caught tuna, dressed simply in lemon and olive oil; or *bruschette*, in which ripe, home-grown tomatoes and home-pressed olive oil produced a little eruption of flavour in the mouth. He has a particular gift: he creates extraordinary, brilliant, life-affirming parties.

We went on foraging expeditions, to collect wild caper berries on the rocks of Antipaxos. On the cliff-tops above the village of Lakka, we found the feathery leaves of wild carrot and thyme so powerful that stepping through the undergrowth released a living potpourri. To prepare for a festival, Spiro would take me on gastronomical treks. First we would go to buy the best chickens, then to find a cache of much-prized Antipaxos wine. Finally we would climb above a hill-top village to Katerina's house. I was taken aback by clothes lines strung across her garden, on which fluttered what seemed to be macabre linen shrouds, dancing in the wind. They were lengths of muslin, washed and pegged out to dry after she had made fresh cheeses in them.

For many years, Spiro had been taking people on guided walks; one summer he began to give enchanting cookery lessons, first with barbecues on the tiny beach at Marmari, then at a magnificent olive press in the hills. These most informal of master-classes were followed by a feast. Elias and Antonis played bouzouki and mandolin; Ourania sang. Nothing was faked for tourists; gradually, the locals themselves came. One winter, he rented the school hall to demonstrate ancient recipes – to the locals. Families across three generations turned out to hear Spiro celebrate the old ways: the uses of herbs and fresh ingredients. If there is any knowledge, insight, warmth or colour in these pages, I owe it to him.

———

There is a ghost flitting across these pages … Archduke Ludwig Salvator, traveller, conservationist, anthropologist and artist, who lived on Paxos in the 1880s.

What a lovely man: I wish I had known him. He had an insatiable curiosity about *everything*: houses, agriculture, fishing; he noted down lullabies and children's games; birds, bees, marriage practices … His sketches, reminiscent of Edward Lear, show us Paxos as it was – and still is, in tantalising places. Thanks to a recent, enchanting translation of his book into English, we know much of the Paxiots' lives.

People who live on islands have something quirky about their characters. The Paxiots can be bafflingly 'laid back', staring gloomily for days as rain drips through a ceiling… until the roof falls in. Punctuality is optional. Young and old, they are spontaneously demonstrative towards small children: even teenage boys, usually too self-conscious about looking cool, will hug toddlers affectionately. When roused, the men can erupt in towering rages, soon blown over, like October storms. A few are cynical, intuitive, elegiac and romantic, and there is a spark – a bit of island magic – in them. Why else, as the Archduke records, would they have created a word for a Tuesday Lizard – a *Triti Youstera*?

THE RECIPES

I have two confessions to make.

First, the recipes in this book have *not* been selected because they are historical survivors of ancient peasant cookery – though many of them are. I have selected them because they are wonderful: forthright and honest, allowing their ingredients to speak simply and clearly for themselves. They are all about making something taste as good as it can be: masterpieces of simplicity. Although these dishes can reach gastronomic heights – in some, you will find a balance of flavours so delicate that it would satisfy a Michelin-starred chef – that is simply the outcome of a tender love for, and understanding of, their ingredients.

Secondly, I also hope, rather timidly, to suggest ways to keep these traditions alive. This involves a very presumptuous proceeding indeed: I don't think these recipes should be preserved like musty museum pieces. They should be brought into the knockabout world of the modern kitchen. So I have made it clear which are the original 'peasant' recipes, as told to me; and I have also tried new ways of putting this knowledge to good use today, using the originals to create fresh dishes that are true to the spirit, if not the letter, of the old. In the process, I hope that I have produced recipes that today's cooks – no matter where they live – can try themselves. You should be able both to serve the traditional classics for friends and family, and try some of the modern recipes, which you could, if you so wished, serve to guests at a smart dinner party in London, Sydney or New York.

If the ancient ways are so valuable, why mess about with them? Because no recipe stands still. When cooking, it is your own adjustment of the ingredients, your manipulation of the recipe to your own taste, that make it your own. That, of course, is how recipes were handed down: always with slight variations, like a strengthening of the gene pool. In the old recipes we have the survival of the fittest for its purpose; and each generation has its own contribution to make. This is mine.

Does it matter? Of course it does. Food is our most fundamental means of communication; of giving life and expressing love.

It is that important.

FIRST THINGS FIRST...

MEASUREMENTS

Many of the old recipes have never been written down and are often very approximate. Ingredients are used as they come to hand. It is also difficult to render measurements across the imperial, metric and US cup systems; you are advised to keep strictly to one system within a recipe.

COOKING TIMES

Ovens and their temperatures vary enormously – think of something wood-fired outside in the garden and the latest convector oven. Let your senses guide you; unless you have items in the oven that might collapse if it is opened too early, check on what is going on. A golden colour that indicates it might brown too much, if left without a foil cover till the end of the cooking session; a sizzle or bubble, which indicates that the contents of a pie are cooked and piping hot; and above all your sense of smell. Cultivate these senses and you will gain confidence in the most odd kitchens.

MEANS OF COOKING

Cooking without an oven is the ancient way. Braising food in a pot on top of a stove, or a fire, is a marvellous way to cook; as you stir, your eyes and your nose tell you whether the dish is good and ready. Many older Greek housewives use pressure cookers to tenderise stews, reduce the long cooking time and save energy; as there are now fewer of these in our kitchens, I give guidelines for slower cooking in the oven.

OLIVE OIL

Olive oil is the star of this book: it is quite simply the elixir of life. Do not use extra-virgin olive oil for cooking; its very virtues – a strong, grassy, richly mineral flavour – make it too overpowering. Nor is it healthy to use it repeatedly as a cooking medium; olive oil used for frying should be thrown away after first use. All recipes in this book specify 'light olive oil' for frying or other cooking purposes. Using your very best extra-virgin olive oil for these mundane tasks is a waste and could spoil your dish. For frying or roasting, rapeseed, sunflower or fresh vegetable oils can be substituted.

Cooking is like learning to sail a boat. When you know the basics – how to trim the sails, read the direction of the wind, adjust the tiller – then you can make your own voyages. Just set sail ...

CHAPTER 1
FOR STARTERS: *MEZEDES*

Mezedes *are my favourites of all Greek dishes. From ancient times, drinks were always served with small morsels of food. Although the name* mezze *or* meze *apparently originated in Persia, then spread across the Ottoman empire, when served as little dishes with drinks, these delicacies are also still known by their ancient name,* oretakia, *from* orexi, *meaning appetite – they are literally 'little appetite-whetters'.*

Simple and unpretentious, they are the sort of dishes you don't tire of – a yoghurty, astringently garlicky tzatziki *scooped up with a hunk of very fresh bread; the smokiness of aubergine (eggplant) in* melanzanasalata; *a glorious mouthful of tomato, garlic and basil, glistening with flakes of sea salt and extra-virgin olive oil on a bruschetta … this is what I am happy to eat again and again. As a rich American who lived for six months in a luxury hotel in London that had sold its soul to 'fine dining' once confessed to me, 'After a while, it kinda makes you sad.'*

These, on the other hand, are dishes whose very lack of complication makes you feel that all is right with the world. At their best, they will restore your love of life.

TZATZIKI

Believe it or not, there are two *sorts of* tzatziki. *On Paxos, it is an appetizer; I have heard it described as 'hot': it's supposed to ignite your senses, not cool them. Garlic has an assertive, warming role. It is finished with fresh dill, for astringency; not mint, which tends to be cooling, like the* raita *that accompanies Indian dishes. This is done by eye and by taste, so quantities are always approximate.*

SPIRO'S PARTY TZATZIKI

1 garlic bulb, to taste

sea salt to taste

1 water glass extra-virgin olive oil

1 large or 2 small cucumbers

1 kg (2 lb) full-fat Greek yoghurt

1 tablespoon white wine vinegar

lots of chopped fresh dill

freshly ground black pepper

To make your *tzatziki* – the 'hot' sort – start the day before by chopping garlic cloves, pounding them with salt, and letting them steep in the olive oil in a screw-topped jar. This allows the flavours to infuse and the oil to 'cook' the garlic, taking out its bitterness and softening it so that when eating it you do not, as Spiro describes it, come up against 'rocks in the road'.

Carefully wash the cucumber, to clean the skin of any chemicals or waxed surface if it is shop-bought, not home-grown. Then grate it through the largest holes on your grater and salt it. Leave to drain for an hour then tip the cucumber into a clean tea towel or piece of muslin and squeeze out as much water as you can. Mix the yoghurt with the white wine vinegar, olive oil and marinated garlic to taste; allow the flavours to mingle, covered in the fridge, for a couple of hours. When ready to serve, stir in the cucumber and dill for colour and freshness. This prevents the *tzatziki* from splitting if left too long combined with the cucumber before you serve it. Season with pepper.

Note: to serve *tzatziki* alongside roast lamb as part of a main dish, ease up on the amount of garlic, use less of the olive oil, very finely dice your cucumber and add chopped mint leaves instead of dill.

FRESH CUCUMBER, MINT AND DILL MOUSSE

This is tzatziki *transformed into a simple, refreshing mousse. It is very light and innocent of garlic: serve a slice with very good smoked salmon as a starter, or present it garnished with dill as part of a medley of* mezze.

MAKES ABOUT 6 SLICES

½ cucumber

5 gelatine leaves

400 g (14 oz) Greek yoghurt (full-fat or 2% fat)

handful of mint leaves, very finely chopped

1 dessertspoon finely chopped chives

1 tablespoon finely chopped dill, plus a few fronds to garnish

zest of 1 lemon

squeeze of lemon juice or a splash of white wine vinegar

sea salt and black pepper

Grate the cucumber and leave it for half an hour, lightly salted, in a sieve over a bowl, pressing down occasionally with the back of a wooden spoon to remove the juices. Squeeze out any remaining water before using.

Place the gelatine in a glass with water to soften (follow pack instructions). When soft, heat in a small saucepan with a little water until dissolved. Put the yoghurt with all the remaining ingredients in a separate bowl, season to taste and fork it through to mix thoroughly.

Add in the gelatine and mix further; pour this into a small tin, dariole or jelly mould – I use a miniature loaf tin – and refrigerate for 3 hours or overnight.

When ready to serve, carefully immerse the tin or mould in hot water, taking care that it does not seep over the rim, and after a few seconds it should loosen so that you can turn it out onto a plate. Garnish with fronds of dill.

RUSTIC HOME-MADE *TARAMASALATA*

This is natural and rough-textured – you can taste the extra-virgin olive oil in each lovely, salty morsel. It is as far away from that lurid pink paste sold in plastic tubs as it is possible to get. Spread it on toasted bread and hand round on trays with olives as a generous canapé. Otherwise, place a bowlful in the middle of the table and watch your guests' exhilarated expressions, as they dig in to the real thing.

SERVES 4

100 g (3½ oz) stale white bread, cut into rough slices, crusts removed

250 g (8 oz) white *tarama* (or half pink and half white *tarama*) or 250 g (8 oz) smoked cod's roe

1 medium onion, peeled and finely minced or grated

3 tablespoons freshly squeezed lemon juice

150 ml (5 fl oz/⅔ cup) extra-virgin olive oil, plus a few drops to garnish

30 g (1 oz) parsley, chopped

Greek olives and thick slices of rustic bread to serve

Place the bread in a bowl with just enough water to cover and soak it for 10 seconds, then squeeze out the water; you do not want the bread to disintegrate – it just needs to be moistened.

Using a pestle, blend together the bread, *tarama* or roe, onion and lemon juice. Then gradually add the oil in a very thin trickle until thoroughly combined. Some people (myself included) simply work this mixture through with clean fingers.

Sprinkle in the parsley, then shape the mixture into a mound and arrange on a plate or in a bowl, garnished simply with just a few drops of the finest extra-virgin olive oil. Serve with thick slices of bread that has been lightly toasted.

Note: *tarama* is fish roe from cod, striped mullet, carp, herring or other fish, that has been preserved in salt. Top-quality *tarama* is creamy-coloured roe – which is the most expensive; bright pink roe is cheaper and often artificially dyed. Many Paxiot cooks combine the pale or 'white' *tarama* with the pink, or use smoked cod's roe, to improve the appearance of *taramasalata*. Delicatessens and Greek food specialists usually stock *tarama*; if not available, use all smoked cod's roe by removing the skin and mashing the roe.

KOLOKITHOKEFTEDES

Pronounced kolokEETHokeftedes, this means courgette balls; surely too unbecoming a name for something so delicious. For me, the perfect recipe for these golden, feather-light fritters, which burst in your mouth with melting cheese and fresh mint, was the Holy Grail. One hot fritter would make a perfect starter, with minted yoghurt and some lemon on the side; two or three, a vegetarian supper.

MAKES ABOUT 8

2 large courgettes (zucchinis)

100 g (3½ oz) feta

100 g (3½ oz) *kefalotyri* or Cheddar

zest of 1 lemon

2 tablespoons cornflour (cornstarch)

handful spring onions (scallions), very finely chopped

handful flat-leaf parsley, very finely chopped

large handful fresh mint leaves, very finely chopped

3 teaspoons dried oregano

1–2 eggs

lots of black pepper

vegetable or sunflower oil, for frying

Trim the ends from the courgettes then grate them using the second to largest holes on your grater, into a wire sieve lined with muslin (or a clean tea towel) and leave to drain for 10 minutes. Then gather the grated courgette up in the muslin and squeeze strenuously: you will find that you can remove lots more liquid. Leave the courgette to dry naturally for a couple of hours. Grate the cheeses and scatter over the lemon zest and a tablespoon of the cornflour.

Take a large bowl and mix the courgettes and cheese mixture with the spring onions, parsley, mint and oregano, grinding black pepper into the mixture as you go. Break an egg into a small bowl, beat thoroughly with a fork and add to the mixture. Stir it until the mixture begins to stick together. If it is too dry, add a second egg. Roll into balls, about the size of a golf ball, then leave in the fridge for an hour or two to firm up. When ready to cook, roll each ball in the remaining cornflour.

In tavernas, these would be plunged into a deep-fat fryer. If you are shallow-frying at home, you may flatten the balls slightly into the shape of patties, to colour them all over more easily. To cook them, heat the oil in a deep pan, maximum one-third of the way up the sides, to avoid hot fat spitting. Heat until a scant teaspoon of the mixture bubbles and sizzles immediately on contact with the fat. Cook a couple at a time to avoid the oil cooling down; turn over gently with a slotted spoon to ensure they are crisp and golden brown. Drain on kitchen paper before serving, still warm.

RAW VEGETABLES WITH ANCHOVY AND WALNUT BAGNA CAUDA

This is a creamy, walnut-studded version of the bagna cauda *that is popular served with platters of glorious crudités just over the water in Italy.*

SERVES 6

2 large garlic cloves, peeled and crushed in a pestle and mortar

10 anchovy fillets in oil

2 heaped tablespoons capers

1 heaped tablespoon walnuts, chopped

250 g (8 oz) crème fraîche

2 teaspoons white wine vinegar

freshly ground black pepper

Add the garlic to the anchovies and the oil from their tin to a small pan. Over a very gentle heat, mash the anchovies with a wooden spoon until dissolved. Remove from the heat, stir in the capers and walnuts, then stir in the crème fraîche and vinegar. Add a good grinding of black pepper, remove any obtrusive lumps and serve in a warm bowl for people to dip their vegetables. If you have a dish with a small tea light beneath it, or a hotplate, use this so that the vegetables can be dipped into a warm, salty, nutty sauce.

Carrot, chicory, radicchio, peppers, celery, cucumber, fennel, spears of tiny raw asparagus, lettuce, florets of cauliflower – whichever is at its peak of freshness – are all chopped into small batons. Wash them, drain and arrange over a platter.

THYME *CROSTINI*

Olive oil and herb-permeated toasts: take a country loaf, French baguette or slices of ciabatta, and cut thick diagonal slices. Put them on a baking tray in a hot oven for 5 minutes – checking they don't burn – until they are light golden. Pound thyme leaves, some extra-virgin olive oil and a pinch of sea salt in a mortar to release the aromatic thyme into the oil. Using a pastry brush, paint the toasts whilst still warm with this mixture, allowing the thyme leaves to sit on top of the painted side of the toast. Sprinkle with flakes of sea salt. These form a base for *bruschette*; or leave them plain, to dip into the hot, gooey centre of a package of feta, baked in foil in the oven with a little olive oil and herbs.

BRUSCHETTE

BRUSCHETTA WITH TOMATO AND BASIL

A classic: toast or griddle slices of fresh rustic country bread, rub with the cut side of a clove of fresh garlic and sprinkle with your best extra-virgin olive oil. Take ripe tomatoes, cut them into dice, add salt, freshly ground black pepper and olive oil, and allow the flavours to mingle in some fruity extra-virgin olive oil. Top the *bruschette* with the tomato mixture and tiny fresh basil leaves.

BRUSCHETTA OF FRESH MARINATED ANCHOVIES WITH BALSAMIC AND ROCKET

Proof that a rustic dish can be rather sophisticated. Tiny fresh anchovies are split, their spines removed and marinated in oil with a touch of finely chopped garlic and thyme, then served on top of a toasted thin slice of country bread; it should be so impregnated with olive oil that it tastes like glorious fried bread. On the plate add a ball of fresh rocket (arugula), to cut through any fattiness and give a peppery punch. Aged sweet balsamic vinegar, drizzled criss-cross over the anchovies, will add sweetness and depth.

BRUSCHETTA OF TARTARE OF TUNA WITH CUCUMBER, LIME AND CORIANDER

Combine one finely grated onion, 100 g (3½ oz) finely diced cucumber and 250 g (8 oz) finely diced tuna in a bowl, and add a few drops of Tabasco (hot pepper sauce) to taste. Add a tablespoon of little capers and a squeeze of lime juice. Season with a grind of black pepper, then add a few drops of extra-virgin olive oil, and mix. Serve quickly before the tuna begins to lose its colour, in spoonfuls on top of thyme crostini, with chopped coriander (cilantro) leaves on top.

BRUSCHETTA OF FIGS, MIZYTHRA CHEESE AND GREEN LEAVES

Lightly sprinkle thyme crostini with a flake or two of sea salt, bite-sized pieces of *mizythra* cheese (or you could use soft goat's cheese or bufala mozzarella), little slices of fresh fig, some rocket (arugula), a fragment, perhaps, of lemony sorrel leaf and drizzle over aged sweet balsamic vinegar, topped with droplets of very good olive oil.

SKORDALIA

Using a pestle and mortar is a comforting thing. As Patience Gray observes in her inspirational book Honey from a Weed, *pounding fragrant things like garlic, basil or parsley is a tremendous antidote to depression: 'It produces an alteration in one's being – from sighing with fatigue to inhaling with pleasure.' In these days of machines that whizz ingredients into a tiny paste or powder in seconds, this seems odd advice; but anyone who has put something delicate in a washing machine will know how the brutal efficiency of the operation can destroy it utterly. This 'slow is better' maxim is also true of the action of salt on garlic in a mortar, where olive oil can gradually be added with potato for a sublime skordalia.*

SERVES 6

5 garlic cloves

1 teaspoon sea salt

extra-virgin olive oil to taste

4 medium potatoes, peeled and cut into quarters

juice of 1 lemon

Crush the garlic cloves with the salt in a large mortar with the pestle and add a little olive oil so that it forms a paste. Boil the potatoes until soft, and drain them, then add the cooked potatoes one at a time, blending well.

Add the lemon juice then add more oil a little at a time, until you have a thick, glossy paste; taste as you go – you have enough oil when it glistens in the mixture but does not overpower the taste.

Note: if made instantly in a food processor the consistency can swiftly become like glue; it will not take long by hand and it is most rewarding. When storing in the refrigerator, wrap in clingfilm or foil, as the aromas are penetrating.

In the modern kitchen *skordalia* can be used, with a tiny pinch of saffron if you wish, as an *aioli* swirled at the last minute over a fish stew or fish soup, to give a good zing; as a dip with fresh bread, some black olives and some crisp, feisty radishes; or instead of mayonnaise, with hard-boiled eggs or seafood.

THE ULTIMATE RAW TOMATO SOUP

*This is an elixir: delicate and fresh. It is so simple that it hardly requires a recipe.
Unlike the cold Spanish soup gazpacho, it is innocent of green peppers, cucumber, garlic,
vinegar, olive oil, croutons and ice cubes; and it is kept at room temperature, so that the
tomatoes' taste is uninhibited by refrigeration. First, bite into one of your tomatoes. If you
experience a rush of fresh, explosive flavour, don't mess around with it! Forget cooking it,
reducing it, drying it or adulterating it. When home-grown tomatoes are in season and you
have a glut, this raw soup allows a really good tomato to express itself.*

SERVES 6–8

Pour enough boiling water over 2 kg (4 lb) ripe tomatoes in a bowl to cover them. After a minute
drain them, rinse in cold water and slip off their skins. Chop roughly and transfer the flesh in
batches into a sieve – then simply push the flesh through the sieve into a bowl with the back of a
wooden spoon, wiping the underside of the sieve to ensure all the tomato pulp goes into the bowl.
Occasionally you will need to remove the seeds and pith that have accumulated in the sieve. You
will have a soft, pure, pale red liquid; add a teaspoon of sugar if your tomatoes are not very ripe,
and a good pinch of salt. Keep at cool room temperature, so as not to destroy the exquisite aroma
and flavour, stir to mix and serve in small bowls. Add just a drizzle of extra-virgin olive oil and
some tiny leaves of fresh basil; hand round a pepper mill.

Note: you can also oven-dry tomatoes with a little salt, some thyme and olive oil, in a very low
oven. You can use the result for a soup or for tossing over pasta. The flavour is more intense,
because the juice has been condensed – but that is not what this recipe does: it is tomato uncooked
and unadorned. If you find it is separating and a little watery, simply skim off any excess watery
liquid and stir the bowl before serving.

CHILLED SOUP OF CANTALOUPE MELON WITH LOBSTER

Clean-tasting luxury: this is made from simple rustic ingredients, which have all the impact of a restaurant dish.

SERVES 2

1 small lobster

1 large or 2 small ripe canteloupe melons

2 limes

extra-virgin olive oil

aged balsamic vinegar

Prepare the lobster as per instructions on page 260, leaving the tail meat whole to be sliced horizontally in medallions to serve. Halve and remove the seeds from the melon(s), catching all the juice. From one half, dice the flesh and set aside. Spoon out the rest of the flesh and blitz it in the blender to a foamy purée, and pour into bowls. Leave covered in a cool place.

Juice the limes and sprinkle the juice over the lobster meat. When ready to serve, stir the soup then place place bite-sized pieces of the lobster around the edge of each bowl, with the diced melon in the centre. Finally dress the plate with tiny droplets of olive oil and balsamic vinegar. (You can use the leftover lobster with the remaining lime juice and some finely chopped chilli in a little salad; keep the lobster shells for stock.)

Serve with an iced glass of rosé for a summer lunch, or as a pure, refreshing start to a grand dinner.

AVGOLEMONO

This wonderful, life-enhancing froth of a soup contains no salt at all; the lemon juice does the trick. It's a bowlful of beautiful simplicity – and the better your home-made chicken stock, the more glorious. It serves four in small bowls, or two with a bowlful and seconds. Do not heat the froth in the pan once the stock and lemon have been added, to avoid the soup splitting. Use real chicken stock: poach a chicken in plenty of water with a bay leaf, celery, carrots, peppercorns and parsley. The chicken can follow as a main course with boiled vegetables, traditionally served with olive oil and lemon juice dressing; if you wish, extract a little meat from the chicken, dice it finely and add it to the soup.

SERVES 4

500 ml (16 fl oz/2 cups) hot fresh chicken stock

40 g (1½ oz) basmati rice

juice of 2 large lemons

4 large eggs, separated

freshly ground black pepper

Strain the chicken stock into a pan and keep it hot. Soak the rice in water to remove any starch and then add it to the stock in the pan. Bring to the boil and simmer to cook it, so that the flavour envelops the cooked grains of rice. Mix the juice of one of the lemons with enough hot stock to fill a teacup and then set the cup aside.

Beat the egg whites with an electric whisk until they reach soft peaks in the bowl. Add the egg whites to your food processor and, mixing, gradually dribble in the juice of the other lemon; then add the egg yolks, one by one, and then finally the cup full of lemon juice and stock. Whisk or blend to a pale yellow froth.

Take the pan containing the stock and rice off the heat. Gently dribble stock from the pan into the frothy mixture, whisking as you go. Finally, stir this frothy amalgamation back into the pan containing the remaining stock and rice, and stir quickly together, with an up and down movement to keep in as much air as possible. Have warm bowls ready and serve immediately (using a ladle to share out the rice) with a black pepper mill on the table, for people to serve themselves.

CARPACCIOS

Venetians' love of carpaccio *is shared by the islanders; watching Spiro deftly slice a piece of raw fish, add a squeeze of lemon, flakes of sea salt and droplets of oil from his own olives, one realises that raw food has a much longer history than the Venetian occupation. This is simply a hunter-gatherer's snack that had been swimming only an hour before…*

For those who see Greek food as heavy-handedly rustic, these carpaccios will be a revelation. They prove how very simple things can reach gastronomic heights. So great is the respect for very fresh ingredients that this is 'cooking' at its most delicately and exquisitely balanced. I first had a carpaccio *of salmon made by Miltos Arvenis at Vassilis' Taverna in Loggos. He also produced an unforgettable* carpaccio *of white fish with wild plums. I have attempted to reproduce this with some further suggestions of my own. Once you get the hang of combining tastes and textures, you can experiment – and one cannot hold it against these dishes that they are so very, very pretty.*

CARPACCIO OF SALMON WITH ORANGE, CHILLI AND VODKA JELLY

SERVES 4

juice of 3 large oranges

1–2 tablespoons vodka, to taste

½ teaspoon chilli powder to taste

4 leaves gelatine

600 g (1¼ lb) very fresh raw salmon fillet

dill fronds to serve

sea salt and extra-virgin olive oil to garnish

Juice the oranges into a small bowl. Gradually add the vodka and chilli powder, mix thoroughly and taste – you should just discern the vodka, and get a taste of warmth from the chilli. Immerse the leaves of gelatine in a little cold water until they are soft; squeeze them out. Pour the orange mixture into a small saucepan, add the gelatine and stir very gently on a low heat until dissolved. Take a small cake tin which you have lined with clingfilm and pour in the orange mixture to a depth of about 1 cm (½ in). Put in the refrigerator for six hours, to set.

Place the salmon fillet in the freezer, wrapped in clingfilm, for 20 minutes – this makes it easier to slice wafer-thin. Arrange the sliced salmon fragments on plates. Turn out your orange jelly and cut into little squares; dot them around the salmon, add some dill fronds, dress with a few flakes of sea salt and scatter droplets of extra-virgin olive oil over the dish.

CARPACCIO OF TUNA WITH BLOOD ORANGE AND CAPERS

SERVES 4

400 g (14 oz) very fresh tuna

2 blood oranges – if not in season, use navel oranges

2 teaspoons capers – or whole caper berries, chopped

extra-virgin olive oil

1 tablespoon dill fronds

salt and black pepper

Place the tuna in the freezer for 20 minutes, wrapped in clingfilm, to firm up before slicing wafer-thin. Using a sharp knife, cut off the ends of each blood orange and then cut off the peel and pith and slice fine segments of orange, gently removing pips as you go. Save the juice.

Using a very sharp knife, slice the tuna into thin bite-sized slices. Arrange them on plates with a sprinkling of capers and orange segments; top with a little chopped fresh dill, some drops of the reserved orange juice, salt and pepper and droplets of your finest olive oil.

CARPACCIO OF SEA BASS WITH FRESH CHERRIES AND ROCKET

SERVES 4

400 g (14 oz) sea bass

juice of 1 lemon

16 cherries

large handful fresh
rocket (arugula) leaves

sea salt

extra-virgin olive oil

Although I have used sea bass here, you could use halibut or another firm white fish – the freshness is the key ingredient. Place the sea bass in the freezer for about 20 minutes, wrapped in clingfilm, to firm up; then slice it wafer-thin into fine bite-sized fragments, no more than 5 mm (¼ in) thick.

Squeeze a little lemon juice over the morsels of sea bass then lay them out, evenly distributed, on 4 cool plates. Shave little slices off the fresh cherries and distribute them over the plates; top with small rocket leaves, flakes of sea salt and little drops of extra-virgin olive oil.

CARPACCIO OF SCALLOPS WITH BASIL AND LEMON TEARS

SERVES 4 AS A STARTER

4 large or 8 queen size scallops

juice of 1 lemon, and 1 lemon, halved

½ teaspoon sugar

extra-virgin olive oil

small basil leaves

sea salt flakes

Put your scallops in a sealed bag in the freezer for 15 minutes to get firm – do not forget them! – so they are easier to slice thinly. Put half the lemon juice and zest in a small bowl with the sugar and a pinch of salt; cover this with clingfilm, and chill. Once the scallops have firmed up, slice into wafer-thin slices, then toss them in the lemon juice mixture.

When ready to serve, take the slices out of the marinade and spread them over 4 chilled plates, so that you have a wide circle of carpaccio in the centre of each plate. Sprinkle over droplets of very fine extra-virgin olive oil, a little lemon juice, sea salt flakes and some tiny leaves of basil. Prise out a segment of the halved lemon and with the tip of your knife, tease out the tiniest complete fragment; what have you got? The answer, for the Greeks, is a tear. They love these citrus-filled fragments, which burst on your tongue as you eat. Scatter a few tears over the scallops as they go to table.

CHAPTER 2
PIES! PIES! PIES!

The Greeks are pie mad. Toddlers take their first steps to reach out for a pastry; office workers stop to buy a pie for breakfast on their way to work. They are the companion to the labourer's cigarette break, the simple lunch and the giant celebration dish, which lights up faces round the table ... This is possible because the Greeks' notion of 'pie' is extremely elastic: they can be little triangles of crackly filo; huge tray bakes, portioned out with a knife; or hand-held pastries that are sweet, savoury, or a winning combination of both. There are pitas *that are special to each town, island, village and cook – many are family heirlooms. Classics like cheese or spinach pies are the subject of much discussion: everyone is highly pie-opinionated. But it is also an opportunity to take whatever ingredients are best, freshest and in season at home – and experiment.*

The mill grinds all you throw into it.
PAXIOT SAYING

TYROPITAKIA
LITTLE CHEESE PIES

Serve these tiny hot cheese pies as canapés or as part of a mezze. *They are absolutely delicious: crackly, crisp pastry, out of which oozes cheese, with a hit of hot chilli. Mix crumbled feta with a little Greek yoghurt, to bind it, and mash with a fork with a sprinkling of ground nutmeg, to create a filling. Add a drop of Tabasco (hot-pepper sauce), finely chopped mint and black pepper in each parcel.*

Preheat the oven to 200°C/400°F/gas mark 6 and defrost frozen filo (phyllo). For small triangles – canapé size – cut a sheet of filo lengthwise into strips 5–6 cm (2–2½ in) wide. Work quickly so that the dough does not dry out and crumble. (If it is drying, I use a fine water spray, the sort you use to mist over plants.) With a pastry brush, paint the strip with melted butter. Place a heaped teaspoonful of filling at the narrowest end, then fold the bottom edge of the strip to form a triangle, as if you were folding up a flag. Then fold the triangle back on itself so that you continue along the strip, finally tucking in the last edge. Seal the folded edges with a brush stroke of beaten egg. Note: shop-bought filo is usually 30 cm (12 in) long, so you should get 5 strips; I have allowed for wastage, from cracking or broken pastry. If you are doing tiny pies, you may not need to roll them up the whole length of the filo strip; four layers of pastry on the pie is enough. Note: the pies can also be frozen and brought up to room temperature before baking.

Cover 2 baking sheets with foil, brushed with olive oil. Brush each pie with melted butter and place on the baking sheets, ensuring they do not touch. Bake for 15 minutes or until golden brown. Leave to cool for a minute, as the baked cheese will be molten.

SPIRO'S *TYROPITES*

Like all Spiro's recipes, this makes massive quantities, but you can scale them down.
Ourania cooked dozens for guests in the garden, while the music played.

For the pastry, take a kilo (2 lb) of strong white bread flour, 125 ml (4 fl oz/½ cup) of olive oil,
a tablespoon of white wine vinegar, a large pinch of salt and water as necessary. Knead everything
thoroughly into a silky dough, then allow it to rise in a floured bowl, covered with a damp cloth,
for an hour and a half. Then knead it again. Finally roll out a rectangle thinly, and cut this into
half (as illustrated above). Onto each rectangular half, place a mixture of feta (finely crumble the
cheese – allow a dessertspoonful per portion); chopped parsley; mint and other herbs from your
garden, with lots of pepper. Roll it up like a long cigar with the cheese mixture inside; then twist
and knot the ends so that you have a ring, like a joined croissant. Fry these very briefly in hot clean
vegetable oil until crisp, then drizzle with honey, and scatter toasted sesame seeds over the top.
You may need to heat the honey in a saucepan with a little water to make it runny enough to pour.
Serve hot. The sweet, crisp exterior gives way to soft, yielding saltiness …

SPANAKOPITA

A classic spinach pie: this will serve four to six as a main course or twelve as an appetiser.

1.4 kg (3 lb) spinach, stems removed, rinsed, drained and coarsely chopped

2½ tablespoons olive oil

8 spring onions (scallions) trimmed, white and light green parts finely chopped

2 tablespoons chopped fresh flat-leaf parsley

1 tablespoon chopped fresh dill

300 g (10 oz) crumbled feta

3 large eggs, lightly beaten, plus 1 beaten egg for the glaze

1 teaspoon freshly-grated nutmeg

½ teaspoon salt

6 sheets filo (phyllo) pastry

olive oil or melted butter

Preheat the oven to 190°C/375°F/gas mark 5 and lightly oil the bottom of a baking dish about 32.5 × 23 cm (13 × 9 in), or round pan. Place the moist spinach in a large non-reactive pot over medium heat and stir until wilted but still bright green, for a couple of minutes. Drain this in a colander, pressing down lightly to extract most of the water. Add the olive oil and the spring onions to the pot and stir over a medium heat until the onions are wilted. Stir in the spinach, mix well and transfer to a large bowl. Add the parsley, dill, cheese, eggs, nutmeg and salt to the bowl and mix well.

Cut the filo sheets to size to fit the bottom of the prepared baking dish, then place three of the sheets into the base of the dish. Spread the spinach filling over the filo and top with the remaining filo layers. Oil the top sheet and tuck the filo in around the edges, scoring the pastry to make 12 pieces. Brush the top with beaten egg wash. Place the pie in the oven and bake until the top is golden and crisp – about 45 minutes. Cover with foil if it starts to go too brown. When ready, serve right away, or keep for up to 2 days in a refrigerator. Reheat or serve at room temperature.

Note: some cooks add cooked rice, toasted pine nuts or currants to the filling; adapt to your own taste.

LAMB, MINT AND WALNUT PIES

Sometimes one has culinary dreams about how certain ingredients might work together. I fantasised about minced lamb and walnuts, with lots of mint, and packed spoonfuls of the mixture into little pies of puff pastry.

MAKES ABOUT 24 PIES

2–3 tablespoons olive oil

1 large onion, finely diced

1 carrot, very finely diced

1 parsnip, very finely diced

1 teaspoon cumin

1 teaspoon ground cinnamon

2 teaspoons dried thyme

500 g (1 lb) minced (ground) lamb

1 tablespoon quince or redcurrant jelly

100 g (3½ oz) walnuts, chopped

2 handfuls mint, finely chopped

200 g (7 oz) ready-made puff pastry

vegetable oil for greasing

2 eggs, beaten, for glazing the pies

Preheat the oven at 200°C/400°F/gas mark 6. Heat the oil in a frying pan; add the onion and sweat until soft and translucent, then stir in the carrot and parsnip and continue to cook. Sprinkle over cumin, cinnamon and dried thyme, and remove the mixture from the pan; reserve in a bowl.

Add a little extra oil to the pan and then fry the lamb to brown. Season generously with salt and freshly ground black pepper, then add the fruit jelly. When the meat is just cooked through, return the vegetable mixture to the pan and mix thoroughly. In a plastic bag, finely crush the walnuts into little pieces and distribute evenly along with the chopped mint throughout the mince mixture. When thoroughly combined, set to one side.

Roll out ready-made puff pastry on a lightly floured surface and using a pastry cutter cut out a circle approximately 10 cm (4 in) in diameter. Add a spoonful of the mixture, and fold over one side of the pastry circle to meet the other, so that you have a miniature pasty. Carefully seal the edges together, crimping them to make a tight seal. Repeat with the remaining meat mixture and when all the pies are ready, place them on a baking tray covered with foil and smeared with vegetable oil. Ensure the pies are evenly placed on the baking tray, with enough space between them. With a pastry brush, brush the beaten egg over the top of each pie to glaze it and cook in the oven for approximately 12 minutes until they are puffy and golden brown. Serve warm.

PUMPKIN, LEEK AND NUTMEG PIES

The perfect autumnal accompaniment to drinks.

MAKES ABOUT 18 LITTLE PIES

450 g (15 oz) pumpkin

1 large leek

½ tablespoon light olive oil

3 teaspoons freshly
grated nutmeg

freshly ground black pepper

sea salt

100 g (3½ oz) feta

1 tablespoon dried mint

600 g (1 lb 3½ oz) shortcrust
pastry

1 egg, beaten

Preheat the oven to 200°C/400°F/gas mark 6. Peel and dice the pumpkin and finely chop the leek; add to a large frying pan with half a tablespoon of light olive oil, the nutmeg, black pepper and a little salt. Sauté gently and allow to cook down till soft, with the lid on to preserve the liquid – add a spoonful of water if it becomes dry. Do not allow the leek to brown. When the pumpkin is soft, grate feta evenly over the mixture in the pan, sprinkle on dried mint, season further, and stir to amalgamate. Remove from the heat, leaving covered.

Roll out the shortcrust pastry to 5 mm (¼ in) thick, and using pastry cutters – I use 7.5 cm (3 in) diameter – cut out little circles. Lay these on to a baking sheet, which you have lined with foil and painted over generously with olive oil.

Using a teaspoon, put a small spoonful of the pumpkin mixture on one side of each circle, and fold over the opposite edges to create a miniature pasty, sealing the edges so that the filling is secure inside. Beat the egg and using your pastry brush, gently brush all over the tops of each pie, before cooking in the oven for about 10 minutes until golden and crisp.

PAXOS PIE

This is known to the islanders simply as Paxos Pie. It is a pie without pastry – in which milk and eggs are bound into savoury custard with grains of rice. In a pagan celebration of spring, the carnival version of Paxos Pie is made with mint, which has been added to sautéed onions, chopped fresh tomatoes, finely grated carrot, and crumbled feta. For Easter, finely chopped lamb's liver; for spring, broad (fava) beans and their pods, chopped and blanched. In winter, they use dill, spinach and chard – not too finely chopped, so that they can be left in strands, which will bind the pie. Spiro's mother Electra uses octopus and reserves the cooking juices to add to the milk for extra flavour in the pie. In the early days of Venetian rule, owners of plantations of olive trees used to rent them out to poor men, who would collect the olives, process the oil and deliver it to them, together with a pie as a symbolic gift. This is the most comforting of dishes, which each cook happily adapts over time; the sort of truly home-made, make-do dish that becomes a fond childhood memory.

SPIRO'S MEAT PAXOS PIE

Here's an original recipe – it makes one huge pie to feed about twelve people.

light olive oil

some breadcrumbs

200 g (7 oz) rice

1 kg (2 lb) minced (ground) lamb or beef

2 onions, chopped

4 tomatoes, diced

125 ml (4 fl oz/½ cup) water

250 ml (8 fl oz/1 cup) milk

250 g (8 oz) feta

6 eggs, beaten

salt and pepper to taste

Preheat the oven to 180°C/350°F/gas mark 4 and line a large oven dish with olive oil and breadcrumbs to form a base. Soak the rice. Brown the mince, then add the onion, tomato and the water. Remove from the heat and add the rice and milk. Crumble the feta into the mixture and add 4 of the eggs.

Put into the oven dish and pour the remaining eggs mixed with a splash of water on top. Cook in the oven for 1 hour.

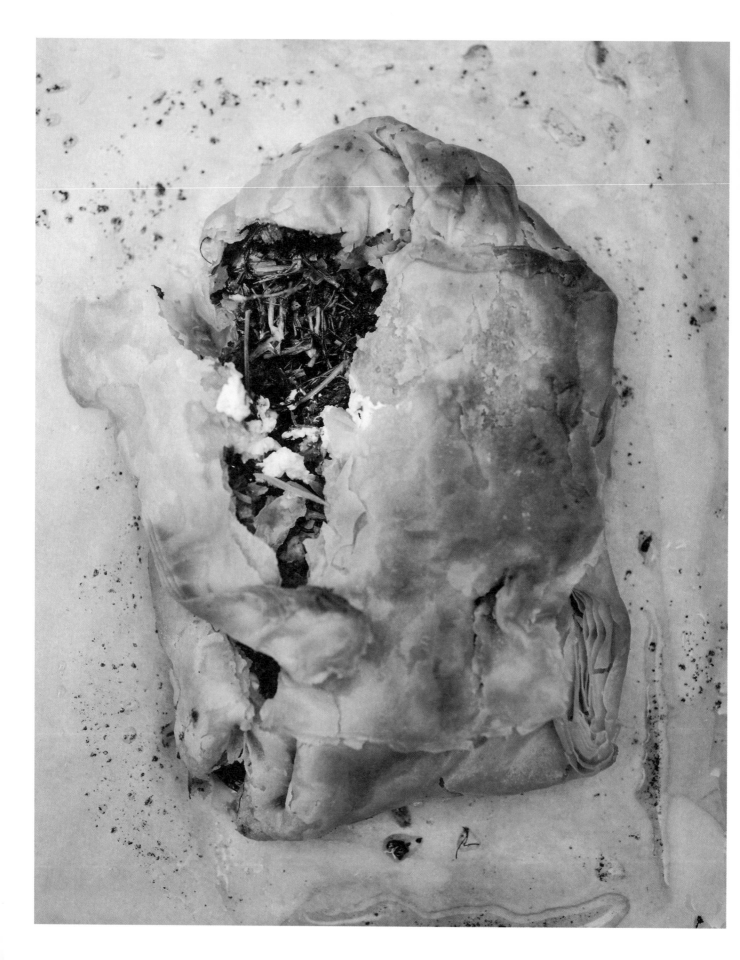

RUSTIC *HORTOPITAS*
SIMPLE WEED PIES

Forget trying to make those elegant little triangles served as canapés – these hot parcels of wild green leaves and cheese can simply be thrown together for a quick lunch or supper, and the more rustic they look, the better.

SERVES 2

Defrost some frozen filo (phyllo) pastry. Pick handfuls of chard, sorrel, spinach, parsley, dill, mint, young beetroot (red beet) or celery leaves, dandelion leaves, nettle tops and wild garlic … whatever comes to hand. Gently melt 200 g (7 oz) butter in a small saucepan; this will be used to paint and seal your parcels.

Add further butter and a little oil to a large frying pan. Chop a handful of spring onions (scallions) very finely, and allow them to sweat. Rinse and chop about 125 g (4 oz) green leaves and herbs, add to the pan and allow them to wilt, leaving the pan uncovered. The steam will rise until they become a dense mass, whilst retaining an intense green colour. Add flakes of sea salt and pepper to taste, then a good grinding of fresh nutmeg. Finally, crumble some feta and sprinkle it generously over the mixture. Take the pan off the heat while you prepare the filo.

Take a double layer of filo pastry, about 15 × 18 cm (6 × 7 in) and using a pastry brush, brush all over the edges of the pastry in a wide band, then place half the mixture in the middle. Add a further three layers of filo pastry on top, painting with butter as you go, and then seal the edges carefully, so there are no leaks – and paint the crimped edges with butter. This is filo for beginners: if you tear the pastry, simply patch, and paint with butter. Repeat for the second pie, and then place both pies gently, using a fish slice to help you, onto a tray which you have lined with baking parchment that has been greased with melted butter – so that the bottom of the pie will sizzle and crisp, too. Bake at 180°C/350°F/gas mark 4 for about 20 minutes – your pies are done when you have an even, deep golden colour.

CHAPTER 3
INTO THE GARDEN: VEGETABLES

The Greek diet is centred, gloriously, around vegetables.

Everyone grows their own; and they do it with pride – in every possible corner of the garden, or on balconies. Barrels, buckets, and old feta cheese tins are pressed into service to increase domestic productivity; derelict wooden boats may be hauled up on shore and filled with earth for a herb garden. Protein, in the form of meat, is relished sparingly; especially now that money is as tight as it was in much, much earlier times. But hardship brings culinary rewards; the following recipes show how in fact this can be an opportunity, not a restriction.

We start, as our ancestors did, with pulses.

FASOULADA

This very plain soup of dried beans was once the daily dish on which every poor man subsisted. It is painful to record that at the time of writing this book, Greeks are queuing in line in Athens at emergency food stations, to be served this subsistence soup, which their ancestors would have recognised.

SERVES 4

450 g (1 lb) dried haricot beans

150 ml (5 fl oz/⅔ cup) olive oil

400 g (14 oz) can tomatoes

1 tablespoon tomato purée

1 large onion, finely chopped

2 carrots, diced

2 celery sticks with their leaves, chopped

sea salt and black pepper

3 tablespoons chopped fresh parsley to serve

extra-virgin olive oil to serve

Soak the beans in cold water overnight; drain, place them in a large pan and cover with fresh water. Bring to the boil, cook for 10 minutes, then drain. Cover again with cold water, bring to the boil again, lower the heat, cover and simmer for 1 hour. Add the other ingredients and simmer for a further 30 minutes or until the beans are tender.

Before serving, add salt and pepper to taste, and the parsley, simmer for a couple of minutes. Serve in warmed bowls, with a little extra-virgin olive oil drizzled over each one, if you have it.

THE BIG BEAN
GIGANTES PLAKI

Just as baked beans on toast are British, so the great gigantes plaki – *giant beans simmered slowly in tomatoes, onion, a hint of garlic, pepper and thyme, perhaps with a squeeze of lemon juice to brighten the tomato flavours – are Greek. This is a great-hearted dish: generous and real.*

Gigantes can be served as a warm stew; or with the liquid reduced, cold and dressed with herbs, as a mezze. *In winter you can serve them on the side with lamb shanks – and, as they are wonderfully satisfying, they can supply the 'meat' in a vegetarian feast. When cooked slowly, they melt in the mouth and there is no chance of indigestion or wind.*

SERVES 4 PLUS

250 g (8 oz) *gigantes* (large white beans)

1 teaspoon bicarbonate of soda

2 tablespoons olive oil

1 large onion, chopped

3 garlic cloves, finely chopped

1 stalk celery and some celery leaves, finely chopped

2 carrots, finely diced

3 large tomatoes, peeled, seeded and chopped

1 tablespoon tomato purée

3 bay leaves

1 tablespoon fresh thyme leaves

2 tablespoons red wine vinegar

sea salt and black pepper

½ tablespoon lemon juice

In a large bowl, add enough water to cover the beans, add the bicarbonate of soda and allow to soak overnight. Bring the beans to the boil over a high heat, cooking for 20 minutes, then rinse them and set them aside in clean water to soak for 1 hour. Drain the beans and set them aside in a colander. Heat the oil in a non-reactive pot, over a medium heat, then add the onion, garlic, celery and carrots, and cook until these lose their crispness. Stir in the tomatoes, tomato purée, bay leaves, thyme and vinegar.

Simmer until the mixture is well blended into a sauce, then add the beans and 330 ml (11 fl oz/1⅓ cup) water and bring everything to the boil over a high heat (do not add salt yet, as it will toughen the skins of the beans). When you have a rolling boil, reduce to a low heat and simmer very gently for about 2 hours, checking every half hour and adding more water if it looks as if it is drying out; the beans should be very tender, with some of their skins breaking apart. When they melt in the mouth, take the pot off the heat, season with salt and pepper, stir in a little lemon juice to 'brighten' the taste. Serve warm, scattered with fresh parsley and some droplets of extra-virgin olive oil.

CHICKPEAS ELECTRA

In Paxos, growing your own is not a lifestyle affectation. Meat is once again special; your daily diet revolves around the staples, and this, especially in winter, makes you long for a little variety. So, sitting with friends and a pack of empty envelopes, pinches of vegetable and salad seeds are shared around.

In winter, the locals have one precious asset: time. Time to cook meals for themselves, rather than for tourists. Time to visit friends for long, circular chats about nothing in particular. Time to tinker with things, in an aimless Greek sort of way; to start building works, which are never quite completed ... while things simmer slowly in the stockpot. There is very little indeed in the shops, so island vegetable recipes are handy. They would be ideal for anyone trying to feed a family well on a hard-pressed budget. As the Paxiots say, 'Turn a miller upside down, and you will find flour for a cake and some biscuits' – with vegetables, you can always make things stretch.

This recipe is a labour of love. Chickpeas, their skins intact, are softened for a day and a half, in a bowl full of lots of clean, pure water. Then remove the transparent papery skin from every one of them by rolling gently in a dry cloth. In a large pot, a finely chopped onion is softened in olive oil until golden. The chickpeas – about 330 g (11 oz) – are added, with at least as much water, and brought up to the boil, and simmered for at least an hour and a half, stirring and topping up the liquid as necessary. Do not add salt at this stage, as it toughens them. Wait until the chickpeas are soft, but still intact, then take three tablespoons and mash them together to make a thick mush; return this to the mixture to form a sauce. Add a wine glass of good extra-virgin olive oil, lots of black pepper, a little salt, stir and serve warm. This is painstaking: ensuring the skin was removed from each one to make it digestible gave me chickpea hallucinations ... it would be done for a special occasion. Luckily, when you taste it, it is a special occasion in itself.

MY BRIAM

This is one of the great dishes of the world: it has the magnificence of simplicity. Briam has Byzantine origins; and is perhaps a cousin to ratatouille. Every bit of flavour from each vegetable should retain its own taste, linked magically through tomatoes and herbs. This recipe is endlessly adaptable. Include whatever is in season – cauliflower florets (added late, to prevent over-cooking), or some finely sliced green beans, for instance. The traditional recipe uses more oil, a great deal more cumin, and sometimes honey. To focus on the delicate taste of the vegetables, the secret is to add them in order of the time they need to cook, treating each with respect, so that they remain separate, and do not disintegrate into a mush. This can be baked in the oven, but I prefer to cook it on top of the stove, so that you can taste and check, as you go.

SERVES 4

olive oil

2 large onions, finely chopped

1 garlic clove, finely chopped

500 g (1 lb) new potatoes, sliced

500 g (1 lb) courgettes (zucchinis), sliced

6 large ripe tomatoes, diced

1 large aubergine (eggplant), cut into discs and diced

2 handfuls mixed flat-leaf parsley, mint and dill, chopped

1 teaspoon ground cumin

1½ tablespoons dried oregano

juice of ½ lemon

feta or goats' cheese (optional)

Sauté the onions and garlic in oil in a non-reactive pan until soft and transparent. Add the potatoes and enough water to cover them generously, then bring to the boil and cover.

When the potatoes are almost cooked, add the courgettes, tomatoes, aubergine and herbs, cumin and oregano, salt and black pepper and continue cooking gently, uncovered, till the liquid is reduced and the vegetables are soft, but still hold their shape. You are aiming for a soupy consistency; the less you stir and break them up, the better.

Check seasoning before serving and add the lemon juice. Serve warm with chopped mint and a drizzle of extra-virgin olive oil on top (adding crumbled feta or goats' cheese if you wish) in warm bowls for supper, with good crusty bread; or, with slightly less liquid, as a vegetable medley to accompany lamb. Leftover *briam* is also delicious tossed over pasta.

Note: to bake this dish in the oven, arrange the potatoes at the bottom of the dish, spread over the vegetables, then cover and bake at 190°C/375°F/gas mark 5, for 30 minutes. Then remove the cover of the dish and bake until the potatoes are tender.

AN ALMOST PERFECT GREEK SALAD

It was an almost perfect Greek salad: bright chunks of freshly cut tomato, bursting with juice. Though each piece was roughly cut – nothing too precise – someone had very carefully and lovingly cut out the core out of each tomato, as this is where any chemicals (should, by chance, they not be organic) will be stored. Crisp, raw onion in mauve-white rings; a generous slab of creamy white feta, sprinkled with dried oregano that still preserves its peppery aroma and its dense green taste. Delicate rings of raw green (bell) pepper; and some of the sweetest black olives you can find. Then superlative, grassy-green extra-virgin olive oil – a real hosanna of an olive oil. Finally you should hear the sound of a serrated knife sawing through the crust of fresh bread into the dough beneath, so that, when you are ready, you can mop up the juices of the fresh tomato and oil ...

Just as you don't mess about with someone you love, so you don't mess about with a horiatiki, *a Greek salad. Forget lettuce, carrots, cauliflower; all kinds of invaders try to make their way into this quintessential Greek dish, but they only interfere with its simplicity. (I think lettuce belongs in a* maroulosalata, *a lettuce salad, which can be awakened by the addition of tiny fresh green herbs.)*

SALAD OF FENNEL AND APPLE

I notice that the Paxiots are very economical with vegetables; if, instead of discarding the crisp white core of a lettuce, you douse it in lemon juice and olive oil, and serve it in little batons, it takes on a delicious new character. The oft-discarded core of cauliflower is highly nutritious and can be used in cooked dishes, or finely sliced, raw, for salads. Here, lemon juice and olive oil 'cook' raw fennel, contrasting with the crisp apple.

SERVES 4 AS A SIDE DISH

2 large bulbs fennel

juice of 2 lemons

2 teaspoons juniper berries, crushed

2 crisp green apples

extra-virgin olive oil

sea salt and black pepper

parsley or chervil to garnish

Chop the fennel bulbs into matchsticks and douse them in the lemon juice. Leave them for at least an hour in a non-reactive bowl, along with the juniper berries, so the lemon juice softens and 'cooks' the fennel. When ready to serve, core and then chop the crisp green apples into matchsticks, toss them with the fennel mixture and some olive oil. Season with sea salt and black pepper, garnish with finely chopped parsley or chervil and serve, dressed with drops of extra-virgin olive oil.

SALAD OF *MIZYTHRA*, ORANGE AND RADICCHIO

The bitter red leaves of this salad work exceptionally well with fresh, creamy cheese and segments of orange – sweet, sour, bitter, salty and crisp on a plate.

SERVES 4

2 handfuls black olives in oil

2 oranges, peeled and segmented

1 radicchio, chopped

1 bulb fennel, finely chopped

1 pomegranate, seeded

3–4 figs, cut into quarters

125 g (4 oz) fresh *mizythra* or Burrata cheese

extra-virgin olive oil

sea salt and black pepper

2 teaspoons fresh thyme leaves

handful of fresh mint leaves, finely chopped

Halve and pit the black olives. In a large bowl, combine the oranges, radicchio, fennel, olives, pomegranate seeds and figs. Scatter the cheese over the top. Dress with extra-virgin olive oil, season with salt and pepper, scatter over fresh thyme leaves and fresh mint.

SALAD OF RAW COURGETTE, GREEN BEANS, LEMON AND MINT

Perhaps the only thing to be said for the summer, if you spend it working for the tourists, is the simply splendid things coming out of the garden: spiky globe artichokes stand sentry beside bushes of fresh herbs; multi-coloured lettuces and bitter leaves; battalions of glossy purple aubergines; the happy yellow of courgette flowers; almost boastful scarlet peppers; and tomatoes, everywhere. Now is the time to gorge on what you can pick.

SERVES 4 AS A SIDE DISH

4 handfuls green beans

2 large or 3 small courgettes (zucchinis), preferably green and yellow

zest and juice of 1 lemon

extra-virgin olive oil

sea salt and black pepper

handful of fresh mint, finely chopped

handful of flat-leaf parsley or chervil

If you have different coloured courgettes, including the bright yellow-skinned, so much the better. Top and tail the green beans, and cut them into bite-sized sticks. Briefly blanch them in boiling salted water for just a couple of minutes, so that they are still *al dente*, then drench them in cold water to stop the cooking process. Drain and reserve.

Cut strips off the raw courgettes with a potato peeler. Mix the courgettes, beans and lemon zest and juice, then toss them in oil to coat the vegetables lightly. Season generously, then garnish with the mint and parsley or chervil.

Note: if you add a few halved cooked baby artichokes and serve this salad with a slice of feta and some crusty bread on the side, you would have a very good vegetarian lunch. The salad is also excellent in a big bowl, with barbecued lamb or grilled mackerel.

STEAMED COURGETTE FLOWERS WITH MELTED CHEESE

Vegetable fritters of all sorts feature in Paxos. Sometimes, however, I long for something that is not battered or fried. So I filled courgette flowers with little dice of strong cheese (kefalotyri or mature Cheddar are excellent) and simply steamed them in a steamer basket for a few minutes. They could be served with a tomato sauce but for something as gentle on the palate as the flowers, pour still-runny scrambled egg around them, so that when you break them open, the melting cheese mingles … a perfect supper for one.

SERVES 1

3 courgette (zucchini) flowers

1 heaped tablespoon finely diced hard cheese such as mature Cheddar

2–3 free-range eggs

sea salt and black pepper

knob of butter

Gently open the courgette flowers and remove the stamens from the centre, replacing them with the cheese. Gently twist the petals together to secure and place in your steamer basket. Fill a pan with water to level with the base of the steamer, put on the lid and bring to the boil. Steam for about 5 minutes.

Lightly mix the eggs together in a bowl, adding salt and pepper. Melt the butter in a non-stick pan and begin to scramble your eggs. Just before they set, remove the steamer basket and very gently lift your courgette flowers into the centre of a warm plate. Pour a halo of scrambled egg generously around the flowers and eat immediately.

FRIED COURGETTE MATCHSTICKS

Can be better than chips. Serves four to six, depending on greed.

900 g (2 lb) courgettes (zucchini) sliced into matchsticks

vegetable or sunflower oil for frying

150 g (5 oz/1 cup) plain (all-purpose) flour

sea salt and black pepper

Spread the matchsticks over a colander, sprinkle with a little salt, and leave to drain for an hour. In a deep frying pan, heat the oil, about 2.5 cm (1 in) deep, until it is very hot. Place the flour in a plastic bag with salt and pepper. Dry the courgettes and add them to the bag in batches, coat them in flour and shake to remove excess. Drop a handful into the oil, being careful not to overcrowd them and turn gently until they are golden. Drain on paper towels, season with salt and serve immediately.

RISOTTO WITH BABY BROAD BEANS, DILL AND OUZO

The key to this magnificent, fresh-tasting green risotto is the quality of the ingredients – use a very good vegetable stock or freshly-made chicken stock, thoroughly strained, if you prefer. Keep the stock hot in a separate pan, on the stove, so that as you add it, it does not impede the cooking process.

SERVES 4

500 g (1 lb) fresh broad (fava) beans

50 g (2 oz) finely diced white onion

50 g (2 oz) butter

3 bay leaves

150 g (5 oz) risotto rice (Arborio or Vialone Nano)

2 litres (3½ pints/8 cups) vegetable or chicken stock

To finish the risotto:

4 spring onions (scallions), finely chopped

2 tablespoons chopped dill

6 tinned anchovies, chopped

stick celery, very finely chopped

1 tablespoon ouzo or dry white vermouth

1½ tablespoons olive oil

100 g (3½ oz) grated parmesan, and parmesan shavings to serve

sea salt and black pepper

Take the broad beans out of their pods, boil them in a generous pan of water with a little salt for 10 minutes then refresh them immediately in cold water. Slip off their skins and leave them to one side.

Sauté the onion in half the butter with bay leaves till soft; add the rice and sauté over a medium heat. Add enough hot stock to cover the rice and leave it to simmer, stirring frequently. As the stock is absorbed, continue to add more hot stock to the risotto, stirring so that the rice becomes thoroughly impregnated. Meanwhile, mix together the spring onions, dill, anchovies, celery, ouzo and olive oil, and blend in a food processor.

When the risotto is reaching *al dente* stage, after about 12–15 minutes, remove the bay leaves. Gradually add the blended paste to the risotto, tasting and seasoning as you go. When the risotto is nearly ready, add the remaining butter, grated parmesan and the broad beans. Stir to warm the beans and serve as soon as possible, with parmesan shavings on top.

BEETROOT

The Paxiots love beetroot – and many of their local ingredients, like feta cheese, lemon juice, olive oil and parsley, suit it beautifully. The fact that it is available when summer fruit and vegetables are over makes it doubly precious. Here is a fresh, lemony beetroot salad with feta; a bortsch-style soup dressed with Greek yoghurt; and an adaptation of a recipe that came originally from Italian chef Antonio Carluccio, for a hot beetroot soufflé with anchovy sauce, which makes a dramatically fuchsia-pink starter worthy of Schiaparelli. Remember that the deep red of beetroot juice will colour the urine of those who eat it, so you may wish to forestall the alarm of those who have indulged.

PANTZAROSALATA TIS BELINDAS
BELINDA'S BEETROOT SALAD

To cook beetroot (red beet) without your kitchen resembling the aftermath of the Charge of the Light Brigade, simply chop off the green beet leaves (you can wilt these down as a vegetable, or use them as salad, later), and leave the spidery tap root at the end and all the skin intact. Place the beetroots in a package of foil, add a little olive oil and seal very securely. Place this in a baking dish and bake in the oven at 180°C/350°F/gas mark 4 for approximately 45–60 minutes until the bulbs are soft when pierced with a knife.

Allow the beetroot to cool and then put on a pair of rubber gloves. You will find that as you hold the beetroots under a running cold tap and rub them with your gloved fingers, the skins simply slip off; put these neatly in the tin foil and place in the bin. You are now left with glistening, deep-red beetroot.

Slice the beetroot into a bowl. Season with sea salt and freshly ground pepper. Crumble over some feta, a handful of crushed wet walnuts, some chopped spring onions (scallions) and a little chopped fennel for texture and crunch; then dress with lemon juice and extremely good cold-pressed extra-virgin olive oil. Scatter over some finely chopped parsley, and a little dill and mint; stir to mix at the table, so that your feta takes on the beetroot juices and turns very pink.

BEETROOT SOUP WITH GREEK YOGHURT

This intense, deeply-flavoured soup looks spectacular with a spoonful of chilled Greek yoghurt.

SERVES 4

1 onion, chopped

1 tablespoon olive oil

500 g (1 lb) beetroot (red beet), cooked, skinned and roughly diced, with chopped leaves

pared rind of 1 lemon (without pith)

1 tablespoon grated fresh horseradish

1 litre (1¾ pints/4 cups) beef, chicken or vegetable stock

juice of ½ a lemon

sea salt and black pepper

Greek yoghurt and chopped chives to serve

Follow the method for cooking beetroot from the previous recipe. Sauté the onion in olive oil in a large pan until soft but not brown; slice and add the cooked beetroot, lemon rind, horseradish and stock and season generously with salt and black pepper. Bring to the boil, then simmer for 15 minutes.

Remove the lemon rind and purée in a food processor until smooth, then return to the saucepan. Add the lemon juice and seasoning. To serve, either reheat, carefully avoiding boiling, or chill; add a generous dollop of Greek yoghurt and chopped chives to the surface of each bowl.

HOT BEETROOT SOUFFLÉ WITH HORSERADISH AND AN ANCHOVY SAUCE

Horseradish – chréno – has been cultivated since antiquity. Apparently the Delphic Oracle pronounced that horseradish was worth its weight in gold. This recipe is for four individual ramekin dishes, 9 cm (3½ in) across; or use a large single soufflé dish, with a slightly longer cooking time.

SERVES 4

400 g (14 oz) cooked beetroot (red beet) (see page 84)

160 ml (5½ fl oz) pink grapefruit juice, or 100 ml (3½ fl oz) lemon juice and 60 ml (2 fl oz) water

1 level tablespoon finely grated fresh horseradish

3 tablespoons plain (all-purpose) flour

4 eggs, separated

25 g (1 oz) butter for greasing the ramekins

sea salt and black pepper

Anchovy sauce:

a knob of butter

1 large garlic clove, roughly chopped

10 anchovy fillets in oil, drained

225 ml (8 fl oz/1 cup) crème fraîche

For the anchovy sauce, put the butter and garlic in a pan, cook gently for a minute, without allowing the butter to burn. Lower the heat, add the anchovy fillets and stir until they have dissolved, then add the crème fraîche and stir to mix. Remove any lumps of garlic, take off the heat and keep warm.

Grease the ramekins with the butter and place them on a baking tray. Preheat the oven to 220°C/425°F/gas mark 7. Put the beetroot, half the juice, the horseradish, salt and plenty of black pepper into a blender and blend until smooth. In a small saucepan, heat up the rest of the juice and mix it with the flour to form a paste, then add it to the blender. Add the egg yolks to the mixture one at a time and blend until everything is smooth. Pour the mixture into a large bowl.

In a separate bowl, whisk the egg whites until stiff and fold them carefully into the mixture, preserving as much air as you can. Spoon the soufflé into each of the ramekins and bake in the oven for approximately 12 minutes; or 25–30 minutes if you are making this in one large dish, depending on how hot your oven is. Do not open the oven until just before the end of the cooking time; remove the soufflés when they are puffy and golden. Serve immediately: encourage guests to make a hole in the middle of each soufflé and pour in some of the anchovy sauce.

CHAPTER 4

HIDDEN IN THE ROCKS: FISH & SHELLFISH

Apparently fewer people like to eat fish or cook it, nowadays. There are admirable attempts to attract people to fish; but sadly these often take the form of fish sealed in pre-packed portions, as boil-in-the-bag items with a ready-made sauce – in the conviction that you will feel more at home with fish, if you never have to touch it at all.

In Paxos, small boys are shown by their fathers how to gather clams, clean and eat them; when there is a catch of a very big fish, they make excited attempts to scale it, before being pushed aside until they are better at it … A little girl gets her fingers into the cavity of a red mullet, pulls out its guts and cleans it expertly, under the approving eyes of her Yiayia, her grandmother. These children will eat this fish themselves: so they come to associate what is raw with pleasure.

If everyone uneasy about preparing fish went to their fishmonger (who will advise, and gladly) and bought something precisely because they had never cooked it before, they might have an occasional piscine hiccup along the way, but after a while, they themselves will be hooked …

THE TALE OF THE LITTLE FISHES…

Marides *are half the size of a sardine, and twice the size of an anchovy.*

We bought about forty of these little silver fish from the fisherman's brightly-painted boat, and brought them to Spiro's mother Electra. Wielding a small knife with astonishing speed, she scraped and descaled each one. She then took some yellow twine and a huge fisherman's needle to stab through the body of each fish, below the tail, so that they can be suspended, tails up, like a silver necklace …

Finally, she spread over a marinade of five whole bulbs of garlic, each clove finely chopped, with handfuls of dried oregano crumbled off its stalks and enough flakes of sea salt to cover the fish entirely. These are covered with foil – as you will be aware immediately of a garlicky aroma – and left somewhere cool or in the fridge, for a day. When you wash off the excess salt, oregano and garlic mixture, it will have 'cooked' the little fish.

In his garden Spiro built a 'cool' fire, of smoke not flames, composed of green twigs and leaves from the mastic bush. An aromatic perfume curled into the air in the smoke. Suspending the necklaces of fish across a pole, far enough away from the fire – which you should keep damped down, and not allow to burst into flame – he smoked them gently. Spiro uses the precious smoked flesh in little balls of rice and herbs, gently fried and served piping hot.

ODYSSEUS' OCTOPUS

When you are diving for octopus, look out for a little pile of shells on the sea bed, where the octopus has lazily discarded the wrappings from his last meal. Remember where you are: local fishermen may remove this evidence, having carefully memorised the location, so no rival will find the octopus before they are ready to catch it. To tenderise a freshly killed octopus, take one small boy and despatch him to beat it against the rocks sixty times – or it can be 'washed' in a circular rubbing motion against a rock, as if rubbed against an old-fashioned washing board, so that it makes suds in the water.

This is a recipe as old as Homer.

Once the octopus has been cleaned (see page 261), it is put in a pan and heated, without any additions, to release and steam off its juices. The liquid steams and evaporates and gradually the octopus turns a miraculous pink, then a deeper and deeper red. Fruity home-made red wine is added, and then home-made olive oil, and the octopus is cooked very, very slowly; as the wine evaporates, a little water is added, and the octopus is covered and cooked until tender with bay leaves, a little olive oil and black pepper – nothing else – for about an hour and a half. Octopus, like squid, can be cooked quickly – but there is a *moment critique* when it turns from tender to hard rubber, and then it needs slow cooking to become soft and succulent again. Here, it turns a magnificent purple …

CITRUS-MARINATED SARDINES OR HERRINGS

I substitute lemon juice for quite a bit of the white wine vinegar the Venetians often used, which I find a little eye-watering. If you find the fillets too acid when marinated, squeeze a little orange juice over them as you serve them. The orange juice miraculously neutralises the acidity and transforms the dish.

SERVES 4

12 fresh sardines, filleted, or 6–8 herrings, filleted

1 tablespoon white wine vinegar

juice of 3 lemons, and the peel of 1 lemon

2 tablespoons whole peppercorns

1 sprig thyme

4 bay leaves

2–3 garlic cloves, finely chopped

2 oranges, sliced

3 tablespoons extra-virgin olive oil

juice of 1 fresh orange

handful small black olives to serve

1 tablespoon chopped parsley to serve

If using herrings, cut the fillets into chunks. Place the fish in a shallow bowl, skin side up, and cover with vinegar, lemon peel and juice, peppercorns, thyme, bay leaves, half the chopped garlic, and one sliced orange. Leave to marinate in a cool place for at least 12 hours, and then remove the sardines from the marinade and wash them gently in a bowl of cool water. Pat them dry with kitchen paper and place on a plate.

Sprinkle with the remainder of the garlic and the olive oil. Taste a little – if it is too acidic for your taste, add extra orange juice. To serve, add slices of fresh orange, black olives, and scatter freshly-chopped parsley on top, with a drizzle of extra-virgin olive oil and orange juice. If you cut the fillets into little pieces, they can be used on a *bruschetta*.

JUST-CAUGHT SEAFOOD SALAD

This recipe is for whatever has been landed in the catch – or is especially fresh at your fishmonger.

SERVES 6 AS A GENEROUS
STARTER, OR 4 FOR LUNCH

12 large prawns (shrimps) or
1 lobster or 8 crayfish tails

24 fresh mussels

12 clams, such as *palourdes*

400 g (14 oz) squid, cleaned, cut
into bite-sized segments

3 garlic cloves, diced

1 red chilli, finely chopped

good quality extra-virgin
olive oil

juice of 1½ lemons

1 tablespoon finely sliced celery

2 handfuls chopped parsley

sea salt and black pepper

crusty white bread to serve

If you have lobster or crayfish, dispatch them humanely (page 260) and remove heads, tails and de-vein them; then clean and de-vein the prawns, using the heads and shells for a good fish stock. Wash the mussels and clams thoroughly, removing any beards from the shells and discarding any that are already open. To prepare the squid, see page 260.

Place all your seafood into a pot of boiling, well-salted water and simmer for 12 minutes, then transfer into a colander and let the cold water tap run through them, until everything is cool. Now the mussels and clams are open, remove one of the shells, so that they are on the half shell in the finished dish.

Sprinkle the garlic and chilli over the seafood, then dress with olive oil and the lemon juice. Toss everything together until it is well-dressed and leave in a cool place (but do not over-chill in the fridge) for about an hour for the flavours to mingle; add celery for crunch, and toss the salad. Scatter with parsley when serving and hand round a black pepper mill for people to serve themselves. Some crusty bread to mop up the juices would be good here, particularly if it is being served as a light lunch, rather than a starter.

SEA BASS WITH LINGUINE AND WILD MUSHROOMS

Sometimes I begin to weary of the almost ubiquitous tomato sauce in which so many Greek dishes are cooked. I long for something lighter, fresher – and this recipe, and the one overleaf, fit the bill: one autumnal, one summery. Substitute other white fish, like bream, if you wish.

SERVES 4

4 fillets of sea bass

2 tablespoons light olive oil

2 knobs of butter

400 g (14 oz) porcini or mixed wild mushrooms, sliced

400 g (14 oz) linguine

a few fresh tarragon leaves

1 bird's eye chilli, seeded and finely diced

squeeze of lemon juice

sea salt and black pepper

Brush the fillets of fish with olive oil and place on a baking tray skin-side up; season with salt and black pepper and roast in a preheated oven at 190°C/375°F/gas mark 5 for about 10 minutes. Alternatively, pan fry the fillets skin-side down in a hot pan with a little olive oil until the skin crisps (about 3–4 minutes) then gently turn over and cook for another 4–5 minutes, depending on the thickness of the fish. Heat the butter and 1 tablespoon of olive oil together and gently fry the mushrooms, seasoning well. In a large pan of boiling, salted water, cook the linguine until al dente, and drain; mix into the mushroom mixture, stirring in the tarragon leaves and chilli. Serve with a fillet of fish on top of each portion and a little lemon juice squeezed over the pasta.

SEA BASS WITH FENNEL AND LEMON AND WHITE WINE

Select a light white wine for this recipe; an oaky Chardonnay might be overpowering.

SERVES 4

light olive oil

2 fresh bay leaves

4 fillets of sea bass

sea salt

1 bulb fennel, sliced

1 onion, finely chopped

1 lemon, sliced

½ bottle light white wine

juice of 1 lemon

fennel fronds, to garnish

Preheat the oven to 220°C/425°F/gas mark 7.

Take a shallow baking dish; pour in a little olive oil and add the bay leaves. Brush the fish lightly with olive oil, and sprinkle with salt. Chop the fennel bulb into finely sliced rings and layer them with the onion, then add the fish on the top. Cover with slices of lemon and pour white wine around the fish. Cover and seal tightly and cook in the oven for 15–20 minutes; check the fish after 12 minutes. Keep the dish covered; if it begins to dry out, heat up a little more wine to boiling then add it to the dish.

When cooked, gently lift the fillets onto warm plates, spoon the pan juices round and sprinkle over the cooked fennel and lemon juice, and fresh fennel fronds.

WHOLE JOHN DORY WITH TOMATOES AND FENNEL

John Dory, Christópsaro to the Greeks, has a black spot on either side of its body – the imprint of the forefinger of St. Peter. It looks like something Jurassic, but the flesh has hints of fresh iodine, like seaweed – and a mild sweetness which goes especially well with fennel. Try not to eat John Dory in midsummer, as the breeding season is from June to August. As with all simply cooked fish, freshness is everything.

SERVES 4

16 cherry or small plum tomatoes

extra-virgin olive oil

a few sprigs fresh thyme

2 bulbs fennel

1 garlic clove, chopped

zest and juice of 1 lemon

150 ml (5 fl oz/⅔ cup) white wine

1½ litres (2¾ pints/6 cups) vegetable stock

25 g (1 oz) butter

1 large John Dory, about 1.25 kg (2½ lb), gutted and cleaned

sea salt and black pepper

black olives, to garnish

Put the tomatoes in a deep frying pan with a little oil and some fresh thyme leaves, salt and pepper, and cook gently until they begin to sag and collapse. Remove from the heat and reserve.

Quarter the fennel vertically and place the pieces in a deep baking dish. Add the garlic and lemon zest and juice, then pour in the white wine and enough vegetable stock so that the fennel is almost submerged. Dot the fennel with knobs of butter, cover with foil and bake at 180°C/350°F/gas mark 4 for an hour, or until soft.

Remove and heat the oven to 200°C/400°F/gas mark 6. Rub a little olive oil all over the John Dory and place the fish in a large ovenproof baking dish and roast in the oven for about 15–20 minutes; look for some white solids emerging from the cuts in the fish – these milky deposits are a sign that the fish is cooked; *take it out of the oven immediately,* so it remains moist and is not overcooked. Bring the fish whole to the table, dressed with the tomatoes and fennel, some olives and some extra-virgin olive oil.

SCALLOPS IN THE SHELL WITH GARLIC

This reminds one of the Paxiots' Venetian heritage: scallops bubbling in their shells with lemon juice, parsley, garlic and breadcrumbs. I use butter, because it suits the scallops; if using oil, it must not be strong in flavour. Serve with bread to mop up the buttery juices.

For a starter, allow 2 large scallops per person, if they are king scallops; if they are little queen scallops, you may increase this to 3. Mix very finely chopped garlic with lemon juice and unsalted butter to form a garlic butter, which you can keep in the fridge, tightly wrapped, to set.

When you are ready to cook the scallops, they should be detached and cleaned, with the veins removed. If you wish, remove the corals too. Put a little of the garlic butter under each scallop, and then some more garlic butter on top. Grate some dry bread into breadcrumbs and put 1–2 teaspoons of breadcrumbs over each scallop, add sea salt and pepper, a drop of lemon juice and scatter finely chopped parsley on top. Line a baking dish or roasting pan with foil and put the scallops in their shells onto it, taking care to arrange them so that they are level and the juices don't run out when cooking.

Heat an oven to very hot at 220°C/425°F/gas mark 7 and cook for about 10 minutes until tender and the juices are bubbling. Be very careful not to overcook – as soon as they are opaque and white, and the butter has begun to turn a bubbling, nutty, golden brown, the scallops are ready to serve.

CLEAR SEAFOOD SOUP WITH MUSSELS, CLAMS AND SAFFRON

This delicate broth with mussels and clams has been clarified; it is a fiddly process, but rewarding. However, if you lack time or inclination, there is something homely and equally appealing about a broth that has been left un-clarified; after all, a few clouds in the sky need not spoil a picnic.

SERVES 4

2 litres (3½ pints/8 cups) fish stock (page 261)

2 tablespoons light olive oil

2 onions, chopped

1 bulb fennel, chopped into 2 cm (¾ in) chunks

300 ml (10 fl oz/1¼ cups) white wine, plus 3 tablespoons for steaming the shellfish

1 lemon, sliced

2 garlic cloves, chopped

4 sprigs parsley

2 large pinches of saffron

100 ml (3½ fl oz) dry vermouth or retsina

200 g (7 oz) mixed mussels and clams

2 small potatoes, cut into 1 cm (½ in) dice

2 tomatoes, deseeded and diced

chervil sprigs to garnish

sea salt and black pepper

Make a fish stock using white fish bones according to instructions on page 261 and strain it through muslin.

Heat olive oil in a pan and gently fry the onion and fennel until soft, not coloured; add the 300 ml white wine and bubble to reduce by half. Add the strained stock, lemon, garlic, parsley, salt, pepper and saffron. Add the vermouth or retsina and cook the liquid for a further 15 minutes. Taste for seasoning and strain through muslin. Then clarify the soup if you wish, according to the directions on page 261.

Prepare the shellfish. Scrub the mussels and remove their beards and scrub the clams, washing thoroughly in cold water. Steam them in a large pan in the remaining white wine until their shells open. Remove most of the mussels and clams from their shells, reserving a few whole for garnish. Discard any still closed.

Gently cook the potatoes in some of the stock; to serve, re-heat the broth gently with the potatoes and add the diced tomatoes. Float the ingredients in the stock in warm bowls, garnish with reserved shells and sprigs of chervil.

BLACK CUTTLEFISH RISOTTO

Some risottos are delicate, almost to the point of being wishy-washy; Costas's cuttlefish version is gloriously inky and sticky and packs a chilli-infused marine punch.

SERVES 4

1 cuttlefish, cleaned and ink sac reserved, or squid plus squid ink, to make 400 g (14 oz)

3 tablespoons light olive oil

1 medium onion, finely diced

½ each of a red and yellow (bell) pepper, finely diced

1 leek, trimmed and diced

1 stick celery, diced, and celery leaves, chopped

1 small carrot, grated

handful parsley, with stalks, chopped

handful fresh dill, with stalks, chopped

200 g (7 oz) Arborio rice

1 litre (1¾ pints/4 cups) chicken or fish stock

½ bottle white wine

1 red bird's eye chilli, diced

Clean the squid or cuttlefish as per the intructions on page 260. Pull the thick membrane of skin off the cuttlefish and chop the cuttlefish and its tentacles into bite-sized pieces: you should end up with about 400 g (14 oz) prepared cuttlefish.

Place the cuttlefish in a large, deep frying pan over medium heat, and allow the pieces to steam, so that they release and lose their juice. When they begin to dry, add the light olive oil and stir continuously, then add the vegetables and herbs. Cook this mixture until the cuttlefish begins to soften; then add the Arborio rice and continue to stir, coating all the grains. Keep your stock hot in a separate pan, so that you can ladle hot stock across to the frying pan as you need it. Add a little stock and a little white wine, and keep stirring; allow to bubble so the liquid is absorbed and the grains of rice swell. Once it has been absorbed, keep adding stock and wine, a ladleful at a time.

When the cuttlefish is tender and the rice is soft but with a little bite to it, add the chilli, stir to mix, and finally add the ink. Stir this in for a thick, glossy-black, aromatic risotto; note that it should still have a loose consistency – you do not want a dry mixture like a pilaf. Serve immediately.

CRAB IN ORANGE JUICE AND ZEST WITH PAPPARDELLE

The chef Miltos Armenis introduced me to this combination in Paxos; his genius for cooking fish has been an inspiration.

SERVES 2

200 g (7 oz) pappardelle

light olive oil

2 bird's eye chillies, seeded and finely diced

6 tablespoons freshly cooked white crab meat

100 ml (3½ fl oz) white wine

juice and zest of 1 orange

1½ tablespoons flat-leaf parsley, roughly chopped

extra-virgin olive oil to garnish

sea salt and black pepper

Add the pappardelle to a large pot of boiling, salted water. Cook for around 4 minutes or until *al dente*. Put a frying pan on a medium heat, add a splash of olive oil and cook the chillies. Next add the crab meat and cook for a minute. Finally, stir in the white wine and orange juice.

When the pasta is ready, drain it thoroughly and add it to the pan; scatter over the orange zest, take the pan off the heat, and toss the pasta and pour it into a large, warm bowl. Dress with chopped parsley, salt, black pepper and droplets of extra-virgin olive oil.

SWORDFISH WITH AUBERGINE, TOMATO AND FETA

Xifías – swordfish – is a mighty carnivore, pursuing little tuna, dorado, mackerel and squid, so their own meat is very filling. There's a difference between the centre of the swordfish fillet and that of the outer edges near the skin; in the centre you have a pale, juicy texture with a slight milkiness; the outer flesh round the skin is softer, with a wood-like grain and a stronger taste.

SERVES 4

1 aubergine (eggplant), cut into
1 cm (½ in) slices

light olive oil for frying

2 large tomatoes, sliced

4 slices of feta

4 swordfish steaks (allow
approx 125 g (4 oz) per person)

juice of 3 limes

handful fresh basil leaves

salt and black pepper

Salt the sliced aubergine and fry gently until soft and golden; reserve 4 large slices on kitchen paper. Quickly pan-fry the tomato slices till just softened; place four discs on top of the aubergine slices and top with a slice of feta – then flash them under a hot grill to melt the feta.

Cut portions of swordfish about 2.5 cm (1 in) thick; I think this is the ideal size for cooking, so that the outer edges are not over-cooked, while the inside has a hint of pink but is not raw. Season and fry them in a hot pan in a little oil, squeezing over lime juice as they cook – the fish should be moist, not breaking up, and very slightly pink in the centre. Serve the aubergine stacks on top of the fish, or to the side, if you wish, with lots of fresh basil.

TUNA SEARED WITH CHILLI, BLACK PEPPER AND FRESH DILL

Tuna is the fillet steak of the fish world; it should be served still slightly pink in the middle. This recipe offers unexpected but delicious crunch, heat and freshness. Serve with a Greek salad, or some roasted cherry tomatoes.

SERVES 4

4 tuna steaks, each about
2 cm (¾ in) thick

light olive oil for frying

1 red bird's eye chilli, finely
chopped

3 tablespoons chopped
fresh dill

1½ tablespoons ground
black pepper

juice of 1 lemon

extra-virgin olive oil for
dressing

sea salt and black pepper

Pan-fry the tuna steaks in a hot pan in a little light oil for 1–2 minutes on each side, depending on how rare you like it. Remove from the pan.

Mix together the chilli, dill and 1½ tablespoons black pepper and press the mixture into the sides of each tuna steak, like a green and red crust; scatter fragments over the top. Dress with lemon juice, a flake or two of sea salt and drops of your best extra-virgin olive oil.

COSTAS'S BOURDETO

Probably from the Venetian, brodeto; *though every country with a seaside has a fish stew-cum-soup. Costas made this with a kilo of* skorpios, *scorpion fish, cleaned but left whole. It was a triumph. If you wish, you may substitute a combination of two red mullet, filleted; six large prawns; and 500 g (1 lb) of mixed mussels and clams – you can still follow the method below.*

SERVES 4–6

Cook 3 potatoes, sliced, in a deep frying pan with light olive oil and add a very finely chopped onion; then add a glass of white wine and boil furiously, so that the alcohol evaporates. Add the pulp, minus seeds and skins, of 4 tomatoes, a teaspoon of hot paprika, a tablespoon of chopped parsley with the stalks, some black pepper and, if you wish, a teaspoon of tomato paste. Cover this with a lid and add a little hot water from the kettle, then simmer until the potatoes are completely soft.

In a blender, add a chopped garlic clove to a little olive oil and blend to make a thick, pungent paste. Add this when your sauce is amalgamated and the potatoes are completely soft. Then place the fish on top of this mixture and poach them while the sauce reduces, so that the fish is moist and perfectly cooked, and stands a little proud of the sauce. Serve in deep, warm bowls.

CHAPTER 5
WILD THINGS

THE DEATH OF PAN

According to the first-century historian Plutarch, one night a boat was sailing through the dark, close to the island of Paxos; most of the passengers were still awake. Suddenly they heard a strange voice, which seemed to be coming over the water from the island. It called, 'Thamus!' 'Thamus!' – which was the name of the captain of the vessel. He remained silent and afraid; but it called again and again. Finally he answered and the voice said, 'Go to the harbour near Butrinto, and announce ... that the Great Pan is dead.'

Thamus did as he was told (Butrinto is on the Albanian side of the Corfu channel, just north of Paxos) and immediately there was wailing of astonishment and grief from all who heard him. The news travelled fast to Rome, where Tiberius Caesar himself called Thamus to come before him. Pan, the god of animals and all wild things; Pan, the hoof-footed piper at the gates of dawn ... all felt shocked and somehow bereft at the death of a god.

But a hundred years later, when the Roman writer and scholar Pausanias toured Greece, he found that Pan's shrines and sacred caves were still visited and revered. And sometimes, when walking alone over the cliffs in the early morning, the sounds of hidden birds and a rustling through the trees make one fleetingly conscious – like a flash across one's peripheral vision – of the presence of something ...

HORTA

Rumps in the air, bent deeply at the waist, women – from widows to very young girls – are to be seen all over the island of Paxos in March and April, gathering the first luscious green shoots of spring. The Greeks have a passion for all these bitter-sweet weeds, known as horta. *Electra and her two friends, both called Nitza, know by sight those which are good for salads or for cooking.*

The ancients loved peppery, bitter leaves and they searched out the bulbs of grape hyacinths, which stud the hillside with miniature patches of blue. Today's islanders love them too, adding spinach, chard, lovage and sorrel.

Famine is within living memory. During the German occupation of Athens in the last war, an estimated 300,000 starved to death; their bodies were collected off the street each morning. So great was the hunger that the hills were stripped bare of wild greens ... war-time was tough on the island, too. Today, when you see strapping teenagers towering above their tiny grandparents, you reflect on the dramatic change in diet. Horta are still treasured. They are free, growing abundantly on hillsides, at the cost of a little stooping to pick them, with no expensive imports by boat.

Radíkia encompasses wild chicories, dandelions and all kinds of bitter leaves. Greeks cook the leaves and shoots of mallow; they look out for wood sorrel and field sorrel. They seize upon comfrey leaves, wild fennel and wild beets, vlíta.

Serve your weeds steamed, tossed in some good olive oil, with lemon tears and lemon zest; wilted, with a little minced garlic, or some olives; buttered, especially if you have spinach and chard, with mint; or chopped, ready for stuffing in pasta, in which case a generous grind of nutmeg would be splendid. Add chopped drained horta *to little pastry tarts, topped with olives, capers anchovies, béchamel or hollandaise ... purists select the finest little leaves for a salad, with a few slices of radish or raw carrot, and droplets of cold-pressed extra-virgin olive oil.*

WILD GREEN SOUP

This can be made from a basketful of leafy vegetables; or, very pleasingly, from the three witches that curse our gardens: nettles, dandelions and ground elder. Pick only the dainty young leaves of the nettles, young ground elder leaves and small dandelion leaves.

SERVES 4

150 g (5 oz) young nettle tops, dandelion leaves and ground elder; mixed with spinach or chard (optional)

2 tablespoons basmati rice

1 litre (1¾ pints/4 cups) vegetable or chicken stock

1 onion, peeled and finely chopped

2 leeks, trimmed, washed and finely sliced

2 stalks celery, chopped

50 g (2 oz) butter

Greek yoghurt to serve

fresh mint leaves to garnish

sea salt and black pepper

Wash the greens thoroughly, using rubber gloves when touching the nettles, and discard any tough stalks. Wash the rice to remove the starch and add to a pan with the chicken stock, then simmer until the grains of rice are soft.

Sweat the onion, leek and celery in butter in a large frying pan; cover and allow to cook gently for 10 minutes, stirring occasionally, until soft, but do not allow it to brown.

Add the rice and stock to the pan, bring it to a simmer and cook for a further 10 minutes. Then add the wild greens, stirring them as they wilt; simmer them until the rice and nettles are tender. Season with salt and plenty of pepper. Purée the soup in batches, re-heat – but do not allow it to boil. Serve in warm bowls with a swirl of yoghurt and a little chopped mint on top.

Note: if kept too long, the bright green colour will be lost, so if you need to make this ahead, prepare till just before you add the greens, and cook them when you want to eat.

FORAGING ON THE SHORE

In February, seemingly without fail, there are ten days of surprising warm weather. The sea is glassily calm; the balmy air suggests, deceptively, that spring has arrived. These are the alkionides meres, *the halcyon days – thanks to Alcyone, for whom Zeus had a passion. When his wife Hera found out, she changed Alcyone into a bird – and Zeus compassionately gave Alcyone ten days of calm weather, in which to lay her eggs … The Paxiots take advantage of this by going down to the seashore to gather limpets, snails and seaweeds. One seaweed is named* oneira – *which means dream; these beautiful green and white weeds float just under the water. They use them for a salad with limpets, and some rice.*

The tiniest limpets are patales – *a great delicacy. They are pure gellified obstinacy to remove, so use the sharp tip of one shell as a lever to prise out the limpet, and swallow it raw, to taste the sea. There are cone-shaped limpets, too; their raw flesh is blended and eaten on top of fried rice.*

SAMPHIRE

We in Britain are lucky enough to have samphire, as the Greeks do; why do so few *appreciate it? It is my favourite wild food. Take a piece of plainly grilled fish, dressed in a little oil, with lemon juice and rock salt in which a few dried fragments of oregano have been pounded. Serve it with a warm dish of* kritamo: *tiny green stems of samphire that have been blanched very briefly, then anointed with a little lemon juice, the very best olive oil, and dressed with some 'tears' of lemon segments … a dish with an incredible depth of flavour. When preserved in white wine vinegar, samphire can be used in winter salads.*

SNAILS

After winter hibernation, snails come out in the spring showers – and are promptly collected by young and old. They are fed only garden greens, to purge them, for a week. At Electra's, they are washed repeatedly in clean, pure water, so that streams of saliva-like suds come from them: not appetising, but extraordinary. When the snails are covered in a great deal of salt, some make a bid for freedom, climbing out of the bowl: we allowed one of the bravest to return to the garden, to relate to friends his horrid experience. Then the whole bowlful is rinsed of salt and boiled with an enormous plateful of fresh dill, parsley, chard, dandelion leaves and chopped spring onions (scallions). No garlic, just olive oil, is added – and this forms a light sauce, leaving a deliciously pure, meaty taste to the snails.

CHAPTER 6
MEAT

Our sense of smell is one of the most intense and emotional of our senses, as those who have lost a loved one can attest – a long-ago perfume; the smell of wood in a workshop … A whiff of the aroma of roasting lamb can suddenly whisk me away to Paxos, as if I were walking through the olive groves.

Lamb is an all-pervasive ingredient of life on the island. Paxiots like hunks of lamb, spit-roasted; slices of roast shoulder of lamb, edged with crisp fat; juicy brown cubes nestling inside pitas; *slow-cooked* kleftiko; *lamb shanks, falling off the bone into a dense, cumin-fragrant tomato sauce; kebabs, sprinkled with oregano and lemon juice; and* paidakia, *tiny lamb cutlets, sweet and pink.*

Whilst lamb is most intimately connected to Greek life, from the whole Paschal lamb on the spit to the simplest kebab, every scrap of beef, pork, chicken and game is also prized; and there is much to respect in the Paxiots' affectionate devotion to offal.

WHOLE ROAST LAMB ON A SPIT

Rub the skin with salt and ground black pepper and pour olive oil over it, which you massage in thoroughly. Prick the skin here and there on the surface with the point of a knife and stick in leaves of rosemary; add slivers of peeled garlic in the pockets next to exposed bone.

Take halved lemons, rosemary, bay leaves, fresh thyme and unpeeled cloves of garlic, and stuff them into the body cavity, which you then sew up with a large darning needle and some un-dyed twine. Thread the lamb on the spit – mechanical if you have one, and secure it so that it turns over the fire. This fire will have been prepared, if it is on a beach, with two long lines of softly glowing white embers with a central gap between them, above which your lamb is suspended. This means that the lamb profits from the heat as it turns, without ever being directly above the flames; there is also space for you to put little trays between the embers, with hunks of bread in them, to catch the juices as they fall; a very good alleviation to a keen appetite, while you are waiting for the lamb to cook. With a little brush made from twigs of thyme and rosemary, baste the lamb with liberal libations of olive oil and red wine vinegar, as it cooks.

In the nomadic way, the meat when ready is simply placed on a wooden block and hacked through with a cleaver; platters of steaming meat are eaten with the hands, and both fingers and face are washed with the help of cut lemons.

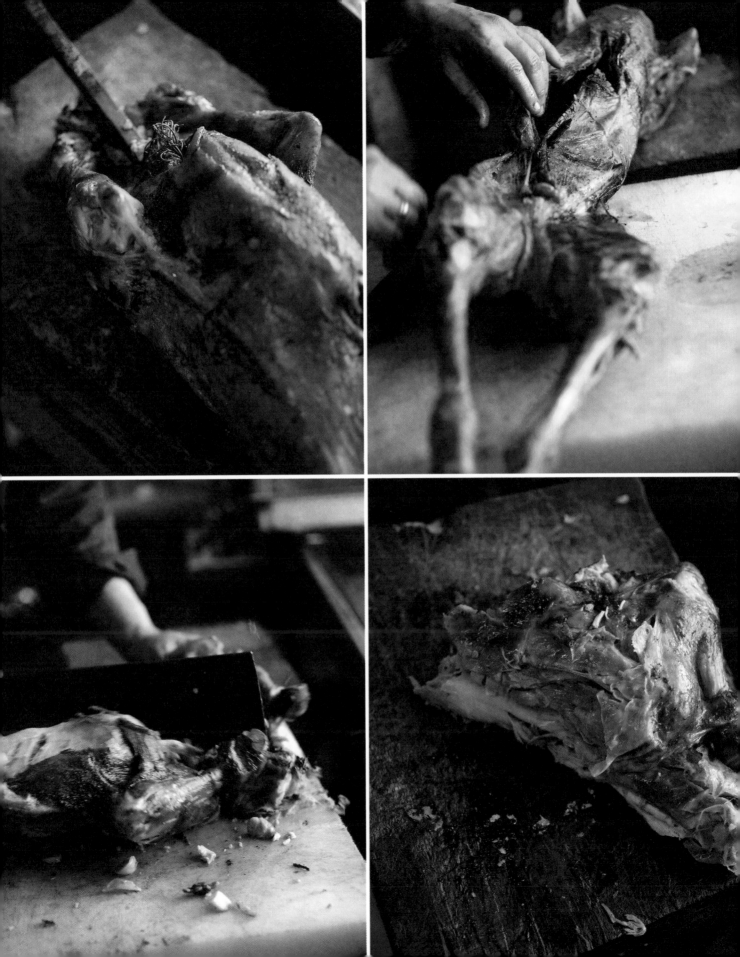

LAMB WITH ARTICHOKES

I had heard about Electra's lamb with artichokes, but had never been lucky enough to taste it. Then I was invited to supper on Christmas Eve … the artichokes had come from her garden, preserved from summer in her freezer; the meat was browned, before going into a pressure cooker. This is my version; it is a good-tempered dish you can keep warm for late guests – and the combination of artichoke hearts with meltingly soft lamb is so unexpectedly good that they may be more punctual in future.

SERVES 4

2 tablespoons light
olive oil

650 g (1 lb 5 oz) leg of lamb,
boned and cubed

6 shallots, whole

3 garlic cloves, chopped

2 bay leaves

½ tablespoon fruit jelly
(e.g. quince or redcurrant)

½ bottle red wine

4 large or 8 small artichokes

juice of 2 lemons

Worcestershire sauce and
Tabasco (hot-pepper) sauce
to taste

handful chopped fresh
dill and parsley to garnish

sea salt and black pepper

Heat the oil in a large frying pan till very hot, add as much lamb as will fit without crowding and brown it in batches. Add the shallots and garlic to the pan and fry gently until golden, then add bay leaves, browned lamb, any juices, the fruit jelly and wine. Bring to a boil then reduce the heat; cover the pan and simmer until the lamb is tender for about 45 minutes (or cook slowly in a sealed casserole in a medium hot oven). Add a little water to keep it from drying out, if necessary.

Boil the artichokes until the leaves come away easily (saving them for a cook's treat with vinaigrette or melted butter). Cut away the choke (page 257) and chop discs of artichoke heart into bite-size pieces; keep in water to which you have added the lemon juice, until needed.

To serve, add the artichokes to the meat and simmer gently; stir, season and add a good splash of Worcestershire and Tabasco sauces; check and simmer, uncovered, until everything is tender and the liquid forms a sauce. Serve scattered generously with fresh dill and parsley.

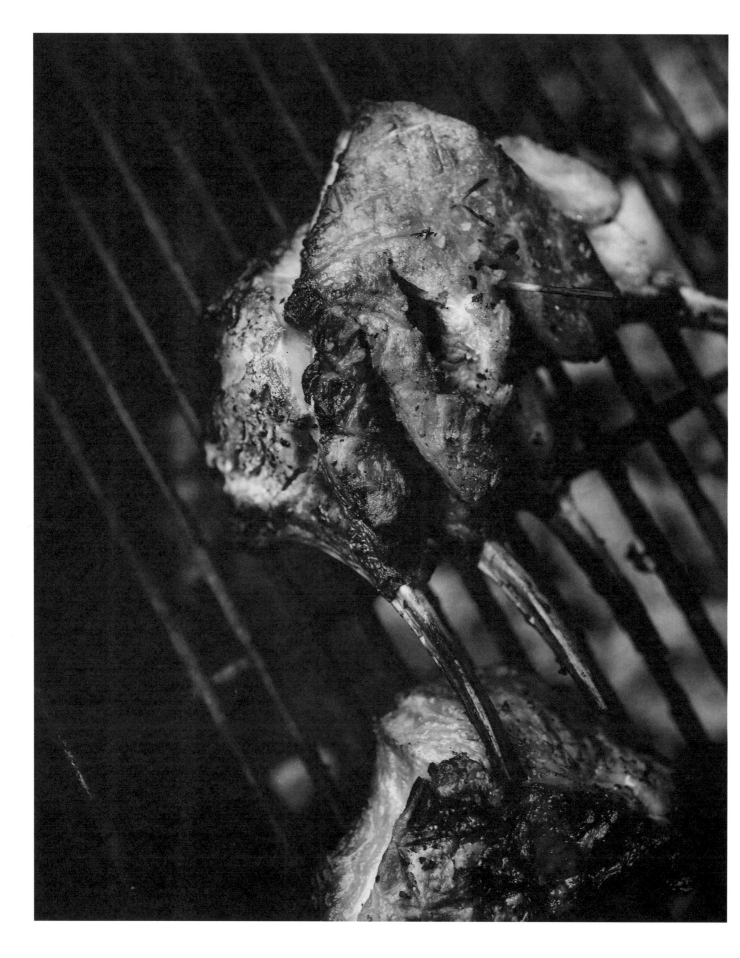

PAIDAKIA
LITTLE LAMB CUTLETS

It is a help to cut a rack of lamb into portions of three or four attached cutlets each, before cooking; you can judge how the meat cooks, and they can be swiftly served to guests without fiddly carving. You can see when the meat is still pink on the inner slices, suit individual guests' tastes, and check you do not over-cook.

SERVES 4–6

2 racks of lamb, French trimmed

3 garlic cloves, sliced

3 sprigs fresh rosemary

light olive oil

sea salt and black pepper

Ask your butcher to French trim your racks, or do it yourself, removing the chine bone. With a sharp knife cut between each cutlet almost to sever them, but not quite, for portions of 3–4 cutlets each. Tuck slivers of garlic and rosemary leaves between the gaps, close them up together and massage olive oil, with plenty of sea salt and black pepper, all over the meat. Leave, covered, in a cool place for a couple of hours, for the flavours to infuse.

To cook, if possible on a charcoal barbecue, wait until the embers are just glowing white. Place on the barbecue for approximately 20–25 minutes; turn them occasionally, so that the outsides brown and crisp. (If you do not have a barbecue, preheat the oven to 220°C/400°F/gas mark 6, so that it is very hot indeed.)

To serve, allow to rest for a few minutes, accompany with *tzatziki* (page 23), or pungent *melanzanasalata* (smoky aubergine purée), and a fresh tomato and thyme salad.

LAMB SALAD WITH WATERMELON, POMEGRANATE AND MINT

I sometimes think leftover cold roast lamb is as good as the original dish.

Take some pink slices of cold roast lamb and lay them out on a platter with pieces of watermelon, add some glistening pomegranate seeds, dressed with a little extra-virgin olive oil mixed with a very little white wine vinegar, to taste.

Add flakes of sea salt and black pepper, with crumbled morsels of creamy feta scattered over the lamb slices before you dress them on the plate, with a few fresh green leaves if you wish. Finally, a generous scattering of chopped fresh mint … this would go beautifully with a side salad of chilled new potatoes, tossed in yoghurt with chopped spring onions (scallions) and chives.

SOUVLAKIA

These miniature kebabs really are tiny – almost the size of Japanese yakitori – and take seconds to cook. Pork is best, as its fat melts deliciously as they cook, keeping the souvlakia *moist; if you use lamb, ensure there is a little fat on each morsel.*

SERVES 4

500 g (1 lb) neck of pork

150 ml (5 fl oz/⅔ cup) light olive oil

juice of 6 lemons

4 teaspoons dried oregano

2 bay leaves, crumbled

sea salt and black pepper

extra-virgin olive oil to serve

good country bread to serve

lemon wedges to serve

Cut the pork into 2 cm (½ in) cubes with a little fat remaining to keep them juicy. Soak a dozen small wooden skewers for an hour in water so that they won't burn (you can also soak rosemary sticks, removing all the leaves except those on the tip).

Mix the oil, 2 tablespoons of lemon juice, half the oregano, the bay leaves and plenty of salt and pepper in a dish large enough to hold all your kebabs. Thread the meat on to the skewers; leave them in the marinade in the fridge for an hour or overnight.

If it is not barbecue weather, I find it best to cook on an iron griddle pan, so the kebabs are easy to turn and have lovely seared stripes. Cook for just a couple of minutes and turn once. Drizzle extra-virgin olive oil over toasted country bread and serve with two or three miniature kebabs per person, sprinkled with the rest of the lemon juice, sea salt, more olive oil and oregano, and lemon wedges. Be prepared to repeat the process, as there will be demands for more …

Some have eaten the pigs and others have paid for them.
PAXIOT SAYING

MILLENNIUM NIGHT SHEPHERD'S PIE

One stormy December I rented a house on the cliffs with Goofy, the dog I had rescued, stacking huge olive logs on the fire for warmth, as the waves crashed onto the rocks below. All the tavernas were closed – but we were not lonely. Greek hospitality reaches its peak at this time: people take it in turns to prepare meals for whoever turns up, sending the message 'I'm cooking' by bush telegraph, so the whole island resembles a rather inebriated itinerant house party. One night, made foolhardy by wine, I volunteered to cook on New Year's Eve …

Would five people turn up, or five thousand? I had some ingredients for moussaka; *I had a feeling the Paxiots might take to shepherd's pie. Great platters of food ready, the dog and I waited … and waited. No one came. Crestfallen, we went to bed – until suddenly I heard a huge crash on the door downstairs. Dripping figures stampeded into the house. I had forgotten how very late the Greeks eat, even in pitch black in winter. Talking, arguing, laughing, smoking, drinking, they fell on the food: this spiced shepherd's pie was despatched in minutes.*

SERVES 10–12

4 onions, chopped

2 garlic cloves, chopped

light olive oil for frying

2 aubergines (eggplants), sliced

2 kg (4½ lb) minced (ground) lamb

2 teaspoons ground cinnamon

2 teaspoons cumin

3 handfuls chopped parsley

1 tablespoon chopped thyme leaves (or ½ tablespoon dried)

1 tablespoon tomato purée

4 chopped, seeded and cored tomatoes, or 400 g (14 oz) tomato passata

½–⅔ bottle red wine

Worcestershire sauce to taste

Tabasco (hot-pepper) sauce to taste

salt and black pepper

For the mash:

2 kg (4½ lb) potatoes

200 g (7 oz) butter to taste

Fry the onions and garlic in olive oil in a large deep pan until soft, then add the aubergines and fry until soft and golden, and reserve. Next cook the mince in batches, turning to brown on all sides. Reserve batches while you cook the next one.

Return all the meat to the pan, season with salt, pepper, cinnamon, cumin, parsley and thyme, then mix in the tomato purée and tomatoes or passata. Add the cooked aubergines and onions; bring to a simmer, stirring, until the mixture is thoroughly cooked through. Gradually add wine over the next 45 minutes to an hour until absorbed, as if you were adding stock to a risotto.

Add Worcestershire and Tabasco sauces, and more salt and pepper, tasting as you go: this dish benefits from strong seasoning. (At this stage, you can leave it to cool overnight in the fridge, then skim off fat congealed on the surface.) If using straight away, ladle off excess fat from the surface, before spreading the meat into a large baking dish. Cook, drain and mash the potatoes with butter, season and spread in rough peaks over the top. Bake for about 30 minutes at 200°C/400°F/gas mark 6 until the top has a golden crust and you can see bubbles of meat juices at the edges.

GLOSSA TONGUE

*When travelling from the mainland in winter, I found Spiro had bought
a present for his mother. Flowers? Chocolates? No – inside one of those
ubiquitous blue plastic bags was an entire severed calf's head, and an
additional tongue. Swinging ominously in its gory plastic bag, we carried it
gingerly back on to the ferry. It was a choppy crossing; we took turns nursing
it, and I began to feel queasy ... but when we devoured the tongue in a
melting casserole with wine and onions (think of braised oxtail, but less gamey
in taste), I forgave it. Why are we such sissies about tongue? Prepared at
home, it is unexpected: subtle and creamy. A whole tongue will make several
meals: serve it in warm slices with a salsa verde, or cherry and chilli sauce; in a
mustard dressing, with walnuts; or slice it wafer-thin with pickled vegetables.*

WINTER CASSEROLE OF TONGUE

Put a whole ox tongue into cold water with a handful of salt in a large pan to soak overnight, changing the water in the morning. Add a small bunch of thyme, a dozen black peppercorns and a couple of bay leaves, 2 onions and 2 carrots, all roughly chopped, and then bring to the boil, removing scum that rises to the surface. Turn down the heat and simmer gently for 3½ hours. When the tongue is cooked, remove it from the pan and peel off the skin.

For the casserole, cut as much cooked tongue as you need; to serve four, allow 150 g (5 oz) per person and dice it into fork-size chunks. In a casserole dish add 150 g (5 oz) butter and a glug of olive oil, and fry 4 roughly chopped onions until soft. Add 3 finely-chopped leeks, 3 teaspoons green peppercorns, 2 bay leaves, 2 wine glasses of white wine and 2 of chicken stock. Bring to the boil and simmer until it is reduced to a thick sauce. Add Tabasco (hot-pepper sauce) – I add 2 teaspoons – and Worcestershire sauce if you wish. Add the pieces of tongue and heat them for half an hour in a low oven; serve with chopped parsley on top and mashed potato.

Note: I often use Tabasco as a liquid form of the red chilli pepper which is a feature of food on these islands. Here, it has two roles: to add warmth to the dish and to counteract any fattiness.

SALAD OF TONGUE, GREEN APPLE, MINT AND POMEGRANATE

A lovely introduction to tongue for those who shy away: cut chunky matchsticks of cold cooked tongue, dress with drops of balsamic vinegar, add finely-cut wafers of tart green apple (over which you have quickly squeezed lemon juice, to avoid discolouring) and pomegranate seeds, with chopped fresh mint; dress with extra-virgin olive oil, sea salt and freshly ground black pepper. Accompany with green leaves, basil and raw chicory as you wish.

A LITTLE LAMB TERRINE

One Easter, there was something I had never seen before, turning on the spit. Chunks of lamb's liver and offal had been stuffed with herbs and garlic, and then tightly bound with strips of intestine into a massive long roll: kokoretsi. *When I bit through a springier version of crackling into the slightly metallic sweetness of the liver beneath, I tasted a rustic banquet of cheap ingredients discarded by kitchens in richer, more wasteful countries. To make your own, you must wash every tube of lambs' intestines painstakingly, inside and out, to make the strips that bind up the outside. It's a fiddly, niffy business. I consulted several Greek recipes; one anonymous author wrote rather despondently* 'it might look disgusting to eat guts and intestines but if you taste it you might start to like it ...' *So I have come up with a little lamb terrine, in which slices of streaky bacon act as wrapping. Serve with Cumberland sauce or fruity chutney and hot artisan toast. If pork is not for you, vine leaves can replace the bacon.*

SERVES 4

1 onion, very finely chopped

½ tablespoon finely chopped
fresh mint

butter and light olive oil
for frying

12–14 slices streaky bacon,
rind removed

3 lamb and mint sausages

80 g (2½ oz) lambs' liver, very
finely chopped

2 lambs' kidneys, very finely
chopped, core and gristle
removed

sea salt and black pepper

Cumberland sauce or chutney
to serve

sourdough toast to serve

rocket (arugula) and fresh chervil
to serve

Preheat the oven to 180°C/350°F/gas mark 4. Sauté the onion and mint in butter and olive oil until the onion is transparent; do not brown. Set aside. Take a small pâté dish; I use a miniature loaf tin 10 × 15 cm (4 × 6 in). Line it with clingfilm, then rashers of streaky bacon, overlapped to form a secure covering, and hang over the sides. Take the sausages out of their casings and layer one third on top of the bacon base. Follow this with lambs' liver, then another third of the sausage meat, then the onion and mint mixture in one layer, then lamb's kidney, and finally the remaining sausage meat.

Wrap the overhanging bacon over the top and cover with more bacon, to seal; bring the clingfilm up over the top. Place greaseproof paper on top, and then wrap tin foil right round to seal. Place terrine in a deep baking tray; add boiling water to come halfway up the side of the terrine. Bake for 50 minutes. Use a skewer to test that the terrine is cooked: the juices should run clear. Allow to cool in the tin, then place a weight snugly on top to weigh down the terrine. Store it weighted like this on a plate to catch any drips, overnight in the fridge. To serve, slide a fine knife round the sides of the terrine, turn out and remove wrappings, and slice.

SPICED BEEF SALAD

'The truth without a lie is like a meal without salt.' *Much Paxiot wisdom comes straight from the kitchen. As the saying shows, they admit the need to spice things up occasionally. In winter, the more affluent Paxiots travel, desperate for a holiday with a bit of sun; they have had to watch the tourists sunbathing all summer while they worked. They return with a taste for spicy food like this Thai-influenced salad, with its brilliant balancing act of sweet, sour and hot. Double up quantities as a main course.*

SERVES 2 AS A STARTER

200 g (7 oz) lean steak fillet, porterhouse or rump

4 spring onions (scallions), finely sliced

1 bird's eye chilli, finely diced and seeded

1 tablespoon coriander (cilantro) leaves, roughly chopped

For the dressing:

1 tablespoon lime juice

1 tablespoon *nam pla* (Thai fish sauce)

1 teaspoon palm or caster (superfine) sugar

1 teaspoon chilli powder

Griddle the steak so that it is seared on the outside, but still rare inside; slice it thinly, diagonally, and set aside. Mix the lime juice, *nam pla*, sugar and chilli powder in a bowl, and adjust it to your taste.

When ready to serve, pour this over the beef, turning the slices so they are evenly coated in dressing. Arrange the beef on a platter with the spring onions, chilli and coriander leaves over the top.

DRUNKEN BEEF

Spiro's drunken beef is made from shin of beef browned in cubes, using 1 kg (2 lb) of meat, a whole bulb of garlic and 5 chopped carrots – and it is cooked with 1½ litres (2¾ pints/6 cups) of local white wine in a pot on the stove top, without a lid, at a ferocious rolling boil. You gradually add the white wine, which the beef 'drinks', becoming increasingly tender.

PARTRIDGE WITH MULLED PEARS

In the nineteenth century the Archduke noted that the lamentable Paxiot impulse to kill birds included herons and cormorants, 'who are hunted although they are bad for eating. Bee-eaters with their magnificent gaudy colours are hunted, even though they are not good to eat.' There was a market for goldfinches, greenfinches, thrushes and turtledoves and swallows were killed and eaten. One of the first conservationists, he also noted that seals had been shot to extinction.

But partridges are in every sense fair game; and the Christmas carol is right – partridges and pear trees go beautifully together.

SERVES 2 GENEROUSLY

2 fresh partridges

4 shallots, halved, or 2 onions, quartered

3 pears, peeled, cored and quartered

300 ml (10 fl oz/1¼ cups) sweet wine or perry (pear cider)

sugar to taste – needed if dry perry is used

3 bay leaves

mulling spices (see note below)

100 g (3½ oz) butter

sea salt and black pepper

Note: for mulling spices, use 2 cinnamon sticks, 2 cloves, fresh root ginger, grated, and 2 pinches of allspice.

With a sharp knife or heavy-duty kitchen scissors, cut along the side of the breast bone and down through the middle of the lower portion of the partridge, so that the carcass is split lengthwise in half. Repeat with the second bird.

Take a casserole dish with a secure lid, add the shallots or onions and pears, then top up with the sweet wine or perry – and a dessertspoonful of sugar if it is dry perry – bay leaves and the mulling spices. Fasten the lid securely, and cook at 180°C/350°F/ gas mark 4 for 20 minutes.

Melt the butter in a large heavy frying pan, season the bird with salt and pepper and gently fry on both sides to colour the partridges golden brown; pop into the casserole to roast on top of the pears for a further 20–30 minutes. Check if the partridge is cooked: insert a skewer to see if the juices run clear. Remove the birds and the segments of pear, and keep warm while you boil up the liquid to reduce to a thicker sauce; or simply spoon a little of the sweet juices over the partridge and pear on plates.

Excellent served with buttered cabbage tossed in thyme leaves with salt and black pepper, and some mash.

ROBIN PIE

'Rouboulopita!' *said Spiro Kacarantsas.* 'Robin pie! My favourite.'

'You don't really *eat* robin?' I asked.

'It is the best meat of all the birds.' His eyes gleamed. 'We catch robins in a special way. You make a little tent of sticks, with two large stones propped against themselves at the entrance, and place some grains of rice at the opening, so the robin is lured inside and the stones fall – trapping him. You may have to wait a day or two. The breast is so good – it takes sixteen robins to make a small pie, and the meat is so precious that we strip the tiniest bits of meat off the rest of the bird for a ragu …'

'Have you never heard a robin sing?' I cried, and shuddered.

'Not recently,' he replied.

'I wonder why,' I said drily.

Here is a recipe to banish all thoughts of robin …

GRILLED QUAIL WITH A SAUCE OF CHERRIES AND CHILLI

In this recipe, the ancient Greeks' fondness for 'fish sauce' – which the Romans also adored – is recreated in the salty Thai fish sauce nam pla. A little goes a very long way, but it fixes the flavours of the chilli, the cherries, and their fresh sweetness in a way that perfectly complements the quail.

SERVES 4–6

8 quail

zest of 2 lemons

extra-virgin olive oil

4 garlic cloves

sea salt and black pepper

sprigs of thyme

For the sauce:

450 g (15 oz) cherries, washed, pitted and chopped

juice of 1 large lemon

1–2 tablespoons sugar to taste

2 teaspoons *nam pla* to taste

2 red bird's eye chillies, seeded and minutely chopped

2 teaspoons balsamic vinegar

Cut the quail in half down the back with sharp kitchen scissors. Massage lemon zest with olive oil into every inch of the quail with your hands; add garlic cloves and scatter sea salt flakes over the surface. Cut the quail further, if you wish, into portions. Allow the lemon zest to infuse into the birds for at least an hour.

Bring the quail to room temperature and grill over charcoal for 8–10 minutes, so that the birds brown evenly (portions will take much less time). If using an oven grill, check that they do not catch and burn close to the heat, or cook them quickly in an oven pre-heated to maximum. When they are done, the breasts should feel firm, and juices run clear from the thighs when gently pierced. Scatter over sprigs of thyme.

To make the cherry and chilli sauce, warm the cherries in a non-stick saucepan with the lemon juice and sugar. Add the rest of the ingredients, plus a pinch of salt. Combine and bring to a simmer, adjusting seasoning to taste.

Serve either as a sauce over the quail, or in a warm bowl, for people to dip pieces of quail into the sauce *en route* to their lips.

CHAPTER 7
PRESERVING WHAT IS GOOD

One of the things we surely need to preserve is the thrifty knowledge of our grandparents: making our own cheese and yoghurt; bottling, pickling, drying and preserving for winter. Traditional economies are practised with skill. Brooms are still made by collecting twigs and binding them; if it is your name day, you may receive a wreath of flowers, rosemary, sage and thyme, which will scent the whole house, hand-made with love by the giver. In the kitchen, chillies are hung up to dry; sage leaves and buds are dried to form bunches of faskomilo, *a mountain tea that is a powerful aid for coughs and colds; fish is preserved following ancient recipes; honey of exquisite purity is collected by passionate bee-keepers, who appreciate its taste – and who understand that bees are a barometer of the natural health of the island.*

When you go into a traditional kafeneion, *you are also helping to preserve what is good: the Greek way of life itself. You will find the old ways are still followed, amid seemingly endless servings of coffee: espressos and cappuccinos from Italy; or muddy-sweet Greek coffees, each with a companion glass of water. There are spoon sweets on tiny dishes to refresh the hot, dusty traveller; vast glass containers of home-made preserves; little glasses of ouzo and local limoncello; and local music punctuates waves of village gossip.*

The crab crawls backwards; that is how he progresses.
PAXIOT SAYING

Where shall we meet? Of course, Bournaos will be open …

It is a café from another time – but it is still vital today. The hand-painted Kafeneion sign BOURNAOS is as Greek as the sunshine which slowly fades it. From inside you will hear the bass growl of men's voices and the click-clack of backgammon and worry beads; it is also the home of good local music. The walls sport a splendid collection of 1950s posters – once again covetable – advertising Papastratos cigarettes; and faded black-and-white framed photographs of heroes, braving eternity through bushy moustaches. No EU zone this: a wooden board proclaims that ouzo is still 2 drachmas a glass. Everything is well-used. Pistachio green paint adorns the wooden panelling above a bare wooden floor. Like the massive verdigris church bell hanging from the eucalyptus tree, the café seems to defy time. Costas, intellectual and gentle, runs it; or perhaps, intransigently Greek as it is, it runs Costas …

SAVOURO
PRESERVING FISH

In the nineteenth century, the Archduke noted how the Paxiots preserved fish by preparing a marinated fish dish called Savouro, *with currants, garlic, rosemary and vinegar. 'The fish are first baked and when the ingredients form a sauce, a little hot oil is poured on. They are put into local casks, and form a handy standby in winter.' Here is the village method: it makes a sensational marinated fish salad.*

A shallow tin is prepared with a bed of chopped rosemary leaves and bay leaves. *Gopa,* fish about twice the size of sardines, are cleaned but left whole, then rolled in flour and fried gently in light olive oil until brown and crisp. Place them on top of the fragrant bed of rosemary and bay; then top with red wine vinegar, finely chopped garlic and currants. Cover and keep in a cool place to allow the magic to happen. Turn the fish once a day for three or four days, as the flesh of the fish undergoes a delicious transformation.

NARANJE

Home-made necklaces of orange peel are hung out to dry on terraces. When cooked in syrup, they taste of marmalade.

6 large Seville or navel oranges

900 g (1 lb 14 oz) caster (superfine) sugar

4 tablespoons fresh orange juice

4 tablespoons fresh lemon juice

500 ml (16 fl oz/2 cups) water

Cut each orange into 8 sections and remove the flesh. You will be left with the rind; roll it into curls, and pierce them with a thick darning needle to which you have attached string or twine. Join the ends, so that you have orange-rind necklaces. Hang these where they can sway in the breeze and dry in the sunshine.

Bring a large pot of water to boil, add the orange necklaces, bubbling briskly for 15 minutes. Drain then fill the pot with fresh water, and return your orange curls. Repeat the procedure. Bring them back to the boil and cook until tender, about 15 minutes, then drain and set them aside.

Rinse the pan and add the sugar, orange juice, lemon juice and water. Bring to a boil and simmer until the sugar dissolves; then add the necklaces. Bring to the boil, then immediately reduce the heat so that the liquid just bubbles over the pieces of peel. Cook this until the syrup coats a spoon thickly and your curls are soft, but not falling apart.

This will take about 30 minutes – if you have a jam thermometer, the temperature would reach 230°C/450°F. Set the pot aside to cool. Remove the strings from the necklaces and transfer the orange curls to sterilised jars; pour the syrup over them and seal.

KATERINA'S CHEESES

Above the hilltop village of Fanariotatiko, Katerina Doui's goats run free. They perch like tightrope-walkers above precipices on the cliffs; they feast on the wild thyme and tough plants on the cliffs and in the olive groves around the village. This is a soil that has never known chemicals; the plants which grow on it are infused with minerals from the salty air of the sea. Like a great burgundy, Katerina's cheese owes much to the combination of terroir *and her own technical artistry.*

Cheese-making is seasonal: the ewes lactate in winter, once kids are born; fittingly, some are raised for the Easter feast. There is plenty of milk – which is lucky, because people make pilgrimages from all over the island to buy some of Katerina's famous mizythra *and her rare, sweet,* fresko tyri, *the simplest cheese of all. Literally 'fresh cheese', a* fresko tyri *comes from full-fat goat's milk taken from her ewes that very day. A litre (1 ¾ pints) will make a cheese the size of a fist, prepared with lemon juice as a starter. After an hour the curds are ladled into fine muslin – which looked like shrouds dancing on the washing line when I first went to her garden; knotted and squeezed and left to drip for five days in the sunshine. There is no salt added – the mineral content of the milk will give it a very light saltiness; I wonder if this might owe something to the goats' ingestion of salt sea breezes.*

Mizythra is better known: it can be used in pies, salads; on bruschette; *and you can take a hunk of fresh bread and spread it with* mizythra *and marmalade for breakfast. Some is put into tins for a year, to mature in the dark, immersed in Katerina's own olive oil. This is* lathotyri, *oil cheese; in the course of a year a faint amber skin develops and it increases in texture and pungency; a piece with a sip of* tsipouro, *a clear spirit from the grape harvest, whets the appetite.*

Half the white milk he curdled, and gathered it with speed
In baskets of woven wicker; and half in pails he stood,
Leaving it waiting ready for his evening's food.

THE ODYSSEY

DAMSON AND APPLE CHUTNEY

Preserving things when they are plentiful to be used in the hard times of winter is of paramount importance. The Greeks do have pickle – known as toursí. *This is my own recipe for a chutney using damsons,* damaskiniá, *which make wonderfully tart chutney; if you cannot find them use plums, with a little less sugar added.*

1.35 kg (2 lb 12 oz) damsons

450 g (15 oz) cored, unpeeled, finely chopped cooking apples

3 large onions, finely chopped

3 garlic cloves, crushed

2 heaped teaspoons ground ginger

450 g (15 oz) raisins

225 g (7½ oz) dried cranberries if available, or use extra raisins

450 g (15 oz) dark soft brown sugar

450 g (15 oz) demerara sugar

1.2 litres (2 pints) malt vinegar

2 teaspoons table salt

2 cinnamon sticks

25 g (1 oz) allspice berries

2 teaspoons cloves

Stew the damsons gently with a little water to prevent sticking and when they are completely soft, force the flesh and juice through a plastic sieve with the back of a wooden spoon, getting as much of the pulp through the sieve as possible. This takes a while, but ensures that you are left with a thick mass of small damson stones to discard.

Return the damson pulp to a large preserving pan, add the apples and onion, garlic, ginger, raisins, dried cranberries if you are using them (or extra raisins), all the sugar and vinegar. Sprinkle in the salt. Add the cinnamon, allspice and cloves and bring to the boil, then lower the heat and let the chutney simmer very gently for 2–3 hours, stirring it, especially in the last hour, to prevent it sticking. The chutney is ready when you can draw a wooden spoon across its surface and it leaves a faint 'path' in the chutney before it returns to a mass.

Pour the warm chutney into hot sterilised jars as full as possible so there are no air pockets left. Cover with a waxed disc and seal with a vinegar-proof lid. Store in a cool cupboard for at least three months before eating.

'Do not mention the D word,' they said. Drachma.

We had gathered in the bar for a gloomy evening drink. Greece was on the brink of bankruptcy; at any moment it might be thrown out of the Euro. The view on the island was that if this happened, the dreaded drachma would be re-introduced; and whilst it would nominally be pegged to the same value as the Euro, it would only be a matter of hours before the drachma plummeted in value. The Paxiots would wake one morning and discover their savings were worth only a third of what they had been the day before; but that their repayments on loans and mortgages were still in Euros – and were now massively more expensive … There was no prospect, on this tiny island, of finding more lucrative employment; it was in every sense devastating. Anxiety etched itself into their faces.

DAMSON VODKA

One small reason to be cheerful.

Wash the damsons free of grit, stalks, leaves and twigs, and pierce each one twice with the sharp point of a skewer or needle. Take a tall, sterilised Kilner jar or preserving jar with a clean rubber seal. Half fill the jar with fruit, then add caster (superfine) sugar to come halfway up the fruit, and fill to the top with good-quality pure vodka. Seal and leave in the dark for 3 months, turning occasionally, then strain into a clean bottle through muslin. I use a funnel lined with a coffee filter paper, for an exceptionally clear result. Store in a cool place for as long as patience allows: it will be remarkably cheering after a year.

ΤΙΜΟΛΟΓΙΟΝ

Καφές	Δρ.	1,30
Κακάο	,,	1,15
Λουκούμι	,,	0,50
Οὗζο	,,	1,50
Κρασί	,,	1,50
Γκαζόζα	,,	2,00
Πορτοκαλάδα	,,	2,00
Κόκα-κόλα	,,	2,00
Μπύρα	,,	2,50

ΠΑΠΑΣΤΡΑΤΟΣ

CHAPTER 8
OLIVE OIL & BREAD

If there is one thing a cook should know about, it is olive oil.

'It all starts in myth,' said Spiro. *'Long before Athens was a city, the region of Attiki was so remarkable for its beauty that the people who lived there – just a small community – knew that of course they were the 'chosen ones'. They were not surprised when the gods themselves became rivals to be their protectors. Athena and Poseidon entered into a competition; to show off his prowess, Poseidon dashed his trident on a rock, and water gushed out. But, as he was the god of the sea, of course it was salty, and my ancestors disdained it. Athena simply handed them a branch from the olive tree: the triple gift of light, medicine and food. She was adopted as their Goddess, and the Athenians made the protection of the olive a law. So highly were olive trees valued, that if you cut one down your fortune was forfeit to the demos, the community. These early people noted how olive oil was a wonderful preservative; how it has medicinal uses; and cosmetic uses, healing and smoothing the skin.'*

'At first the oil was used for lamps; archaeologists can still find ancient examples of these. But there is more: the symbolism of olive oil as a source of light fires up the Greek imagination, in stories, songs and art. At Olympia, in the Temple of Zeus, in about 430 BC the great sculptor Phidias produced a massive statue of Zeus, decorated in gold and ivory. To reflect that white and gold, and increase its aura of heavenliness, the statue stood in a shallow lake of olive oil. Everything would have shimmered gold.'

The world publishes the facts, and we think of it as a secret mystery.
PAXIOT SAYING

Thousands of years ago, the Greeks used a round stone on which to crush the olives; in Paxos you can still see these lying discarded on the hillsides. The stone has a channel carved around its edge, where the oil collected and dripped down into a container. This method progressed in minute steps forward, over centuries.

The enormous circular grinding stones you can see in Ourania's olive press would have been familiar to her ancestors and, astonishingly, this continued right up until the 1930s. Olive oil is the ultimate slow food. Over centuries, the painstaking process of 'cold-pressing' olive oil was perfected. Olives were crushed, put in sacks, and the oil was left to settle, then scooped up with a special shell – a conch with a natural spout – in which the oil could be collected and then poured. It is no wonder that cold-pressed olive oil is so much more expensive.

When you want to know what olive oil to use you need to know the acidity of the oil, the date it was produced, and to look for the right type of container. The container should by preference be of dark green glass. You want to protect it from light, which changes the oil, destroys its flavour and its colour. As Odysseus said to King Alcinous, 'In my cellar, there is the old wine, and the oil.' Odysseus knew that the wine needed to be in the cellar to mature, but fresh olive oil had to be there too: you cannot store oil for long, and it needs cool, dark places to avoid oxidation.

Sunlight will also affect oil's acidity – the fundamental register of whether oil is healthy for you. The low acidity of extra-virgin oil is regulated to no more than 0.8 per cent. This is a low-cholesterol, high antioxidant liquid; scientists are only just beginning to appreciate its properties.

The first olives are green; they exude oil which is a little tart and cloudy. This is an assertive oil, bossy, brimful of personality; it can set off a salad and is glorious eaten with bread in its own right. Some people believe that it has properties as a medicine, even for cancer. This green oil, agoureleo, *has almost no acidity, and is the first and finest oil of all.*

Refined oil is virgin olive oil that is passed through filters to remove the sediment, to what the processors would call 'improve' it. But this has literally been through the ringer. The old olive presses could do a maximum of only three pressings a day. Modern industrial centrifugal pressing can do fifty pressings a day. This pulverises the olives so many times a minute that it irrevocably alters its chemical make-up. Essential amino acids and minerals are lost or compromised, and you have oil which is less healthy and much less delicious – although of course it is cheaper. These oils can be used in baking, or sautéing, as a medium; but not as a taste. You can fry with olive oil – lighter oil, not extra virgin – so long as the oil is used once only. As the temperature goes up, so the acidity can rise by as much as ten times – so throw it away afterwards or it will spoil your dishes, and harden your arteries.

OLIVES

Nowhere in the world am I more conscious of being part of a continuum than in Paxos during the olive harvest. The ancient trees, gnarled into fantastic shapes, blanket the island with green and silver; yet they are a relatively recent arrival. The Republic of Venice took over Paxos in the fourteeth century, and the Venetians entirely transformed the landscape from the sparse, rocky island they had entered.

How did they do it? For the price of a coin ... they offered the islanders one thaler – silver coin – for every olive tree planted. Nothing loath, the Paxiots planted half a million olive trees; when you think that Paxos is only 10 km (6 miles) long, this is astonishing. The creation of terraces of loose rocks, to retain the soil around the trees, followed. The whole look of the island changed; and the canny Venetians knew they would be able to levy taxes on the resulting olives and their oil each year, as a return on their investment.

HEY, HEY!

In the winter, some working men came into the café and I tried to repress a shudder when I looked at their hands. Their cuticles were entirely black, out of which flashed sinister, opaque white nails. At first I thought they had some strange disease. 'It is the olive workers,' explained Spiro, 'you can never get the stain out, all your life.'

In the 1830s, there were over a hundred working olive presses on the island. The Archduke described them sadly but respectfully as 'very primitive'. Usually they consisted of a large round stone turned by a mule or donkey. Two goat horns were placed on top of the press, to ward off the evil eye. The ground-up pulp was pushed into baskets and hand-pressed. He wrote, 'the workmen push with all their might against the pole of the press and accompany their work with a wild "hey, hey!" which resounds in the valleys, day and night, during the winter time. In the loneliness of the nights, a loud blast on a shell horn calls the people back to work ...'

DAWN AT THE BAKERY

It is very, very still. Night things are still on the prowl. I hear the rustle of cats hunting in the bushes. The village is as empty and silent as the little town from Keats's Grecian Urn, as I make my way down towards the sea.

There are no directions to the bakery – you are told simply to follow your nose. Up a stone path until a quaint marking on the wall invites you to round a corner ... It is still too early for the cicadas, but inside the old stone-flagged building, Vassilis is at work. White under his Marcel Marceau mask of flour, he works through the night, in the slow nocturnal marathon that is the life of a maker of bread.

Shafts of dawn light through flour-dusted windows show fine particles of flour and ash from the olive fire burning in the furnace, suspended in the air. Vassilis seems unconscious of what he is doing; he was taught as a boy by his pappous, *his grandfather. This is probably the last bakery on the island to still use the old ways, and to eschew any of the chemicals and modern additives which have devalued and polluted our modern bread.*

The flour used is unadulterated; and there is salt, water, and yeast – the precious maià – *a leaven, fed like a holy flame, which is very, very old indeed.*

There is a dulcet roar from within the furnace. One hears the clink of weights placed on scales; the soft thud of dough thrown onto stone; the clack-clack of old wooden trays, into which the portions of dough are neatly arranged, separated by folded canvas, like a much-pleated sail.

Dough is divided with a baker's cutting tool, then weighed, using ancient scales and a one kilo weight. Rarely does Vassilis need to remove or add dough to make weight; it is measured by eye, as if in a trance. The dough is proved for an hour, then it goes into the oven on those huge wooden paddles.

When they come out of the oven, they have a massive cretaceous crust: tap this and it rings like a bell, so that you know that you are going to bite through the olive oil-dark crust into bread that seems to have a life of its own.

COUNTRY BREAD

It would be foolish to pretend one can recreate the taste and texture of Vassilis' village bread at Loukas' Bakery. It is a living thing: formed of a particular yeast; a variety and texture of flour; and the flavour of fire from seasoned olive logs ... but it is possible to bake very good rustic bread at home in your kitchen. What you want for bruschette *and for dunking into* tzatziki *or* taramasalata *is a robust version of a bloomer, with a crust giving way to soft, springy bread with a proper life of its own.*

500 g (1 lb) strong white bread flour

10 g (⅓ oz) fast-acting dried yeast

8 g (¼ oz) salt

3 teaspoons light olive oil

330 ml (11 fl oz/1⅓ cups) water

Put the flour into a large mixing bowl and add the yeast. Then add salt, 2 teaspoons of olive oil and three-quarters of the water. Stir the mixture round and round, and continue to add a little water until you have gathered all the flour together in a soft mass. Brush olive oil over a clean work surface and knead the dough on it for about 10 minutes, or place it in your food processor with a dough hook; work it so that it becomes smooth and silky. Lightly oil a large bowl and leave the dough in it, covered with clingfilm or a damp tea towel, to rise in a warm place until doubled in size. This may take 2 hours or so.

Cover your work surface lightly with flour, place the dough on it and knock out the air by folding the dough upon itself, time after time, so that the dough becomes smooth. Shape it into a large oval, place it on a baking tray on top of greaseproof paper or parchment and seal the tray in a plastic bag, so that the dough can rise to at least double its size, which will take about an hour.

Heat your oven to about 210°C/410°F/gas mark 7 with a metal baking sheet or baking stone inside. With a pastry brush, paint the top of the loaf with olive oil, to produce a golden finish. Put the loaf into the oven on the preheated stone or baking sheet and bake for about half an hour, until the loaf sounds hollow when tapped with your knuckle on the base. Leave to cool on a wire rack.

ROSEMARY BREAD

This is like focaccia, *only a little sturdier. It consists simply of good ingredients: olive oil, flakes of sea salt and fresh rosemary ... the things you find on a Greek hillside. Have a saucer of your very finest extra-virgin olive oil on the table, to dip hunks of the bread.*

300 ml (10 fl oz/1¼ cups) warm water

7 g (¼ oz) sachet of fast-acting dried yeast

2 teaspoons caster (superfine) sugar

450 g (15 oz) plain (all-purpose) flour

3½ tablespoons light olive oil

2 tablespoons sea salt flakes, and extra for sprinkling

extra-virgin olive oil for brushing on top

1½ tablespoons rosemary leaves

In a small bowl combine the warm water, yeast and sugar; set aside for 15 minutes until it is frothy. In a large bowl, add the flour, make a well in the centre and pour in the yeast mixture, 2 tablespoons of the olive oil and half the sea salt. Stir until combined, then use your hands to bring the dough together in a bowl. Alternatively, mix these ingredients at a slow speed in the food processor, using the dough hook.

Turn the dough onto a lightly-floured surface and knead it for 10 minutes – or use the food processor – until you have a smooth, silky, elastic consistency. Make a ball of dough and place it in a lightly-oiled bowl, cover it with clingfilm and set aside for an hour to rise, to double in size.

Heat the oven to 200°C/400°F/gas mark 6 and brush a baking sheet with a little of the remaining olive oil. Punch down the centre of the dough, turn it onto a lightly-floured board and knead until it has reduced back in size: you are looking for something elastic and not dry. Press your dough onto the pan, cover it with clingfilm – allowing space for it to rise – so that it can prove again for about half an hour. Use your fingertips to press characteristic *focaccia* dimples haphazardly – nothing too regular – into the surface of the dough, then brush the surface with extra-virgin olive oil and sprinkle over rosemary and generous flecks of sea salt. Bake in the oven for about 30 minutes until it is golden – and the bread sounds hollow when tapped on the base.

GREEK LEMON BREAD

Adding lemon to your bread creates a bewitching perfume as it bakes in the oven. Use clean, unwaxed lemons, or wash the skin carefully before zesting. A hint of tartness in the bread makes it particularly good toasted, with unsalted butter and honey. Or use it to make generous doorstep sandwiches: cold chicken tossed in yoghurt with spring onion, salt and mint; tongue and tart chutney; or sliced tomatoes with onion, thyme and extra-virgin olive oil.

450 g (15 oz) strong white bread flour, plus a little to scatter

zest of 4 lemons

a tiny drop of lemon extract (optional)

10 g (⅓ oz) fast-acting dried yeast

150 ml (5 fl oz/⅔ cup) warm water

2 teaspoons light olive oil

5 g (⅙ oz) salt

Mix the bread flour, lemon zest and lemon extract if you are using it, yeast, half the warm water and olive oil together on a slow speed in your food processor, using a dough hook, for 5 minutes. Then add the salt and mix for a further 10 minutes on a faster speed, gradually adding water – you may not need it all – until the dough forms a soft and silky mass. (If you are doing this by hand, knead for a couple of minutes before adding the salt, and knead very thoroughly for about 20 minutes.) Leave it to prove in a lightly-oiled bowl covered in clingfilm for 2 hours at room temperature. After it has risen to double its original volume, shape the dough into an oval loaf, and allow it to prove, inside a plastic bag, for at least an hour at room temperature. When ready, the puffy dough will spring back gently when you touch it. Heat the oven to 220°C/425°F/gas mark 7. Score light incisions across the top of the loaf and scatter a little flour over the surface, then bake the loaf on baking parchment on a baking tray, turning down the oven as soon as the bread goes in to 200°C/400°F/gas mark 6 and bake for 25–30 minutes. Check 5 minutes before the end of the cooking time to see whether your loaf is done – tap the base of the loaf smartly with your knuckle and it should sound hollow. Allow to cool on a wire rack.

Whoever is hungry sees bread.
PAXIOT SAYING

LITTLE FLOWERPOT THYME LOAVES

These are not traditional: they are inspired by the islanders' love of the croissant-style rolls they call croizan. *I make buttery loaves, like miniature brioches, in non-stick flowerpot moulds; you could also use baking tins, muffin-size. Start the dough the day before, as the proving process is long. Warm and herb-scented from the oven, they are lovely. Add finely diced cheese, onion or tiny fragments of crisp bacon as you wish.*

MAKES ABOUT 14 TINY ROLLS OR LITTLE FLOWERPOTS

175 g (6 oz) butter

1½ tablespoons thyme leaves

3 tablespoons warm milk, plus 1 for glazing

2 teaspoons dried yeast

2 teaspoons caster (superfine) sugar

1 teaspoon salt

300 g (10 oz) plain (all-purpose) flour

4 eggs, plus 1 for glazing

Melt a third of the butter in a saucepan and gently sweat the thyme until just soft. Leave to cool, keeping all the butter. Warm the milk to lukewarm in a small saucepan, add the yeast and the sugar and take it off the heat to allow it to begin to work – you will see it bubbling – somewhere warm for 15 minutes. Put the salt, flour and 4 eggs into the bowl of a food processor, add the milk and yeast mixture, and beat with a bread hook, on a slow speed for 10 minutes. Soften the rest of the butter and, with the machine running at a slow speed, add this to the bowl of the mixer, a little at a time. After about 5 minutes, the dough should be smooth, shiny and elastic. Then slowly dribble in the thyme. Leave the dough in the mixer bowl, covered with clingfilm, and set aside somewhere warm, until the dough has doubled in size. Turn out the dough to knock it back, turn it over a couple of times, then cover it in a bowl with a clingfilm and refrigerate it for 12 to 14 hours.

Preheat the oven to 220°C/425°F/gas mark 7. Shape the dough into a ball – a little olive oil on the work surface will avoid it sticking – then when it is perfectly smooth, without crevices or folds, divide the dough into 14 even pieces and roll them into little balls. Place them in your flowerpot or other moulds, then allow to rise again for about an hour and a half. Brush the tops with a mixture of beaten egg and milk, and bake them in the oven for about 15 minutes until the tops are fully golden brown. Serve while still warm, if you can. They can also be sealed up, frozen and re-heated when needed.

CHAPTER 9
SWEET THINGS

BAKING

Bringing sweet gifts, especially for someone's name day, is important.

If it's your party, you don't need to worry about baking a cake. Someone will come bearing something sweet …

Greek cakes are often quite plain, but once cooked they may be drenched in a glistening syrup, which permeates them. As you eat, your taste buds detect gradations of sweetness – from a very sweet topping, to the less honeyed layers below. Experimentation has shown me that you can apply this happy principle by flavouring the syrup to suit the cakes – something sharp and citrussy, with baklava; *a little elderflower cordial in syrup over a sponge with fruit; or a dash of Tia Maria over walnut cake. Remember to be generous with the syrup: it looks too much at first, but a cake warm from the oven will soak it up, and become firmer and more intense in flavour as it cools.*

Sleep, sleep, little one,
Till your Daddy comes
To bring you a biscuit,
To bring you a sweet.
VILLAGE LULLABY

A NEW WALNUT CAKE

Karidopita: it conjures up a picture of Athenian ladies serving squares over conversation; and sturdier cakes, baked in villages by grandmothers. Some recipes use flour; others, paximadia, *which are hard bread rusks, crushed to contribute a crumb. I found it a small step to substitute ginger biscuits; then some chopped stem ginger; finally, to add stem ginger syrup to Tia Maria coffee liqueur, to add another dimension. It makes a moist, dark cake – and a wicked dessert with some crème fraîche or Greek yoghurt.*

100 g (3½ oz) butter, softened

75 g (2½ oz) caster (superfine) sugar

4 large eggs, separated

175 g (6 oz) walnuts

80 g (2½ oz/approx 8) ginger biscuits

1 teaspoon baking powder (baking soda)

½ teaspoon ground cinnamon

pinch of ground cloves

4 pieces stem ginger

2 tablespoons Tia Maria

For the coffee syrup:

125 ml (4 fl oz/½ cup) strong black coffee

2 tablespoons honey

1 tablespoon stem ginger syrup

2–3 tablespoons Tia Maria

Preheat the oven to 180°C/350°F/gas mark 4, then grease a 20 cm (8 in) square baking tin with vegetable oil. Beat the butter and sugar in a large bowl until it is light and fluffy, then add the egg yolks, beating each one thoroughly before adding the next. Crush, or pulse in a food processor, the following: walnuts, ginger biscuits, baking powder, cinnamon, cloves and stem ginger.

In a separate bowl, beat the egg whites until stiff peaks have formed. Pour the walnut mixture into a large bowl, add 2 tablespoons of the Tia Maria and mix. Then fold the egg white into the walnut mixture, a third at a time, very gently, to preserve as much air as possible. Spoon the mixture into the baking tin and spread it out gently, for an even surface. Bake until the cake pulls away from the edges a little and a skewer inserted into the centre comes out clean. This should take about 30 minutes. Set aside to cool to room temperature.

For the syrup, combine the ingredients in a small pan and bring to a boil, then lower it to a simmer until the mixture has reduced and thickened, which should take about 15 minutes. Allow to cool a little in the tin, while you take a skewer and punch holes in the surface, before anointing the top of the cake all over with the syrup. Cover the tin and set it aside for a couple of hours, to allow it to infuse and become luscious and moist.

A CAKE OF WINE-POACHED PLUMS

Cakes made with fresh plums are traditional in Greece; this one, using beautiful plums I found in the market, is something special. I poached my plums in some glorious sweet wine – once, with extravagant abandon, in Tokaji – but any fruity dessert wine will do. I had already served some plums warm, as a simple pudding; then I used a teaspoon to drop little portions of poached plum into a vanilla-scented sponge, to bake in gooey pockets.

For the wine-poached plums:

12 plums

2 bay leaves

3 tablespoons caster (superfine) sugar to taste

1 bottle sweet wine

For the cake:

2 large eggs

175 g (6 oz) caster sugar

100 g (3½ oz) melted butter

zest of 1 orange and 1 lime

200 g (7 oz) self-raising flour

1 teaspoon almond extract

1 tablespoon milk

2 tablespoons baked plum flesh

Halve and stone the plums, and place them in a non-reactive pan with a lid. Add the bay leaves, sugar and wine, and top up with water to cover the plums; gently simmer to poach the fruit over a low heat until soft. Taste for sweetness; add more sugar if needed. Remove the bay leaves and serve as a pudding, with ice cream or yoghurt; but save about 8 halves for the cake.

To make the cake, grease a loaf tin 20 cm × 10 cm (4 × 8 in) and preheat the oven to 180°C/350°F/gas mark 4. Beat the eggs and sugar until they are frothy, then gradually add the melted butter. Add the zest of orange and lime, then gradually beat in the self-raising flour and almond extract. Add the milk, to loosen the mixture. Pour half the mixture into the greased tin and dot with some of the flesh from the plums, drained of the juice; add the rest of the mixture and dot more plums over the top. Bake for approximately 35–40 minutes until the top is risen and golden brown. Allow to cool in the tin, running a knife blade around the sides to turn out.

KÉIK ME BANANA

'Cake with banana' – and a salted caramel sauce.

MAKES ONE 900 G CAKE OR
TWO SMALLER 450 G CAKES

3 eggs

175 g (6 oz) butter, softened

175 g (6 oz) caster (superfine)
sugar

300 g (10 oz) self-raising flour

2 teaspoons baking powder
(baking soda)

2 large ripe bananas, peeled
and mashed

1 teaspoon vanilla extract

1 tablespoon brandy

1 tablespoon milk

For the sauce:

200 g (7 oz) caster (superfine)
sugar

100 g (3½ oz) butter, diced

300 ml (10 fl oz/1¼ cups) double
(heavy) cream

1 heaped teaspoon salt

Let the butter come up to room temperature, so that it is very soft. Preheat the oven to 180°C/350°F/gas mark 5. Line the base of a 900 g (2 lb) loaf tin (or two 450 g/1 lb) and grease the sides with a little butter.

Using an electric mixer, mix all the cake ingredients together in a large bowl; when smooth, pour into the lined tin. Bake in the oven for about 30 minutes for two smaller cakes or 45–50 minutes for the large one, checking after 35 minutes if the top is becoming too brown, in which case, cover loosely with foil. Test with a skewer – if it comes out clean, the cake is cooked. Leave to cool down before removing from the tin.

For the caramel sauce, make sure that both butter and cream are at room temperature before you begin. Take a large, heavy-based saucepan – stainless steel for preference – and shake the sugar evenly across the base of the pan. Put it on a medium heat and allow it to melt at the edges. Gently shake the pan as it starts to turn liquid and golden. Do not stir it – just swirl the pan gently until the syrup has turned a rich, dark colour. Then gently stir in the butter and gradually dribble in the cream, stirring, and finally the salt. Serve warm or at room temperature. A tip when cleaning crusty caramel from your pan: add clean water and bring it up to a simmer, so the caramel lifts and combines with the water and can be poured away.

Turn out the banana cake, cut it into slices and drizzle over a little warm sauce. Note: any leftover caramel sauce can be used with ice cream or baked apples.

THE 'MUFFINS' OF ST FANOURIOS

St. Fanourios is an oddity, even in the weird canon of Greek saints. He is the patron saint of lost things – perhaps because, by a delicious irony, his identity has been mislaid; the Greeks can no longer remember exactly who he was. So revering Fanourios takes a little more blind faith than usual …

If you have lost something – perhaps a ring or a bracelet, or you are simply looking for an answer – you bake a Fanouropita: *a cake to seek the help of the saint. As it is the little, everyday things – like car keys – that seem to go missing each morning, I have adapted this idea into lovely, almond and orange-scented little cakes. Perhaps, like Proust's madeleines, they will prompt the memory.*

MAKES 24 LITTLE CAKES

225 g (7½ oz) caster (superfine) sugar

4 eggs

120 ml (4 fl oz/½ cup) fresh squeezed orange juice

3 tablespoons light olive oil

60 g (2 oz) full-fat Greek yoghurt

1 teaspoon pure vanilla extract

1 teaspoon pure almond extract

zest of 1 large orange

190 g (6½ oz) plain (all-purpose) flour

110 g (3¾ oz) ground almonds

3 teaspoons baking powder (baking soda)

Preheat the oven to 160°C/325°F/gas mark 3 and put the oven rack in the middle of the oven. Using a hand mixer, beat the sugar and eggs until they are pale, thick and frothy, then beat in the orange juice, olive oil, yoghurt, vanilla and almond extracts, and the orange zest. Leave to stand.

Meanwhile, in a separate bowl mix together the flour, ground almonds and baking powder. Gradually stir these dry ingredients into the sugar and egg mixture until they are just blended. Put out muffin or cupcake cases, and almost fill them, then bake them on the middle shelf of the oven, until golden on top – a skewer inserted into the middle of the muffin should come out without moist crumbs attached; for cupcakes this will take 20–25 minutes; muffins 25–30. Note: these can also be made in miniature moulds, like *petit fours*, baked for about 10–12 minutes.

GLYKA DESSERTS

In summer, it's fruit: sunshine-ripened peaches, simply sliced and dressed in lemon juice; figs and apricots straight from the tree. On summer nights, gleaming chunks of cold melon, peponi, *and watermelon,* karpousi, *arranged on a platter; grapes, pomegranates and the strange, slightly slimy interior of prickly pears. In the colder months, one wants something rather more comforting: hot, sweet fritters; custards; a hit of chocolate.*

RIZOGALO

I think of this as 'rice pudding that has gone to heaven'. It is sold in little tubs in pastry shops as a sweet snack. Children who will not eat British rice pudding usually adore it.

SERVES 6

100 g (3½ oz) short grain rice

600 ml (1 pint/ 2½ cups) whole milk, plus 1 tablespoon

300 ml (10 fl oz/1¼ cups) double (heavy) cream

zest of 1 lemon

2 teaspoons cornflour (cornstarch)

2 egg yolks

90 g (3 oz) caster (superfine) sugar

pinch of ground nutmeg

½ teaspoon vanilla extract

ground cinnamon to serve

Wash the rice well and drain it, then bring the milk and cream to a boil in a saucepan and add the rice and the lemon zest. Bring the mixture back to the boil, lower the heat and simmer gently for about half an hour, stirring, until the rice is just soft. Dilute the cornflour in a tablespoon of cold milk, add the egg yolks and stir together over a low heat in a small saucepan, until the mixture is thick. Add it to the rice, with the sugar, nutmeg and vanilla extract, and let it cook over a low heat for a further 5 minutes, stirring continuously. This is to infuse it, not to cook it further; beware of over-cooking. Serve warm, with the top of each portion dusted generously with ground cinnamon.

Rizogalo can also be made 'grown-up' for dinner parties, by adding Armagnac-infused prunes, dessert wine-poached plums (page 192), cherries, poached quinces or rhubarb, as you wish. Perhaps it is best of all when eaten chilled from the fridge as a midnight snack.

POACHED APRICOTS WITH YOGHURT AND PISTACHIOS

The house had a shady, tree-filled garden; a small marmalade cat hunted through the bushes. One hot afternoon, I noticed one of the trees was shaking; a boy was hanging like a monkey from the branches. He was stripping the tree of ripe apricots, which he stowed unapologetically in a bag slung over the handlebars of his scooter, and took away. After searching, I found that he had left just four apricots; this is what I did with them.

SERVES 2

vanilla pod

cinnamon stick

4 apricots, halved, stone removed

zest of half a lemon

pinch of saffron

½ bottle sweet dessert wine

1 tablespoon runny honey

To garnish:

runny honey

fresh pistachios

full-fat Greek yoghurt

Split a vanilla pod and scrape out the seeds; place the split pod and cinnamon stick in a saucepan with the apricot halves. Add the lemon zest and saffron, the dessert wine and honey, and poach gently in a covered pan with a little water until the apricots are tender. Allow the apricots to cool in their juices; remove the vanilla pod and when ready to serve, drizzle honey over the apricots along with chilled full-fat Greek yoghurt over which you have sprinkled chopped fresh pistachios.

WARM FRUIT SALAD OF SPICED QUINCES, PEARS AND FIGS

This fruit 'salad' is served as an autumnal warm compôte, so the spices rise to greet to you; however if chilled, it tastes glorious spooned over yoghurt.

SERVES 4–6

2 bay leaves

1 bottle red wine

130 g (4 oz) caster (superfine) sugar

2 cinnamon sticks

4 long strips of lemon peel

2 cloves

2 pinches allspice

grating of nutmeg

(optional alternative:
1 muslin bag of mulled wine spices)

3 quinces

4 ripe purple figs, halved

3 pears, peeled and cored, in large segments

Bring all ingredients except the fruit to the boil in a pan; simmer to combine the flavours. Rub the furry suede off the quinces, peel them, cut into quarters and scoop out the cores; then cut into 5 cm (2 in) pieces. Put these into the simmering liquid and bring to the boil, then turn down the heat and poach with the pan covered, until the quince pieces are tender; test after 20 minutes with the tip of a knife to see if the fruit is soft. Turn the quinces so all sides take on a deep ruby colour. Remove the pan from the heat, allow it to cool then leave it covered overnight for the spices to work their magic in the quinces.

Next morning, put the pan of quinces back on the stove and add the pears; simmer for 5 minutes then add the figs and continue simmer gently for a further 10 minutes or so, until the pears are tender but retain their shape. With a slotted spoon, remove all the fruit and reserve in a bowl. Pass the liquid through a sieve to remove the spices; return to the pan, and simmer, uncovered, to reduce to a glossy syrup. Pour over the fruit and serve.

Note: for ease, you could replace the cinnamon, cloves, allspice and nutmeg with a muslin bag of mulled wine spices.

COSTAS'S GALAKTOBOUREKO

I watched Costas make this at home one winter evening, at the house he shares with Lilly. I try to avoid superlatives, but this is divine: a tart of wobbly warm vanilla custard, not too sweet, topped with golden filo pastry that crackles, infused with syrup.

SERVES 6 GENEROUSLY

250 g (8 oz) butter, melted and clarified

1 pack frozen filo (phyllo) pastry

2 whole eggs

140 g (4½ oz) sugar

6 egg yolks

80 g (2½ oz) cornflour (corn-starch)

2 teaspoons vanilla extract or 1 large vanilla pod, scraped

330 ml (11 fl oz) double (heavy) cream

700 ml (1 pint 3½ fl oz) milk

zest of 2 large oranges

For the syrup:

300 g (10 oz) caster (superfine) sugar

200 ml (7 fl oz) water

zest of 2 lemons

1 strip of lemon peel

Make the syrup by boiling all of the syrup ingredients for 3–4 minutes and allow to cool. Melt the butter, skim off the solids and keep it warm in a small saucepan. Paint the base of a shallow baking tin 20 × 28 cm (8 × 11 in) with butter with a pastry brush, but sparingly; then do the same with 4 individual leaves of filo to build up a base, leaving filo overlapping the sides. Note: you will be using more filo for the top of the pie, when the custard is ready; keep the reserved filo wrapped up, so that it does dry out and become flaky.

For the custard, beat together the whole eggs and the sugar, then whisk in the 6 egg yolks. Mix in the cornflour, vanilla and cream. Heat with the milk and orange zest, and continue whisking, adding the beaten egg mixture. Keep stirring so it doesn't stick; a low heat will avoid boiling or curdling. When at last your custard is like runny mayonnaise, pour into the filo-lined dish, fold over the overlapping edges of filo, and cover the top with 4 more sheets of filo, each painted with melted butter. Gently score the surface into squares with a knife – do not expose the custard – so it will be easier to portion later. Bake for an hour at 180°C/350°F/ gas mark 4. After 40 minutes, check: if it is going too brown, loosely cover the top with foil and continue baking.

When cooked, take the dish out and allow to settle. Then pour cool syrup liberally over the top. Leave to infuse. Note: opposites attract – if the pie is still warm, your syrup must be cold: if the pie is cool, then add warm syrup – otherwise the two will not infuse properly.

HONEY-BAKED FIGS WITH AMARETTO OR MASTIKA

SERVES 4

8 large or 12 medium ripe figs

3–4 tablespoons Amaretto di Saronno liqueur or Mastika

1 teaspoon runny honey per fig

Preheat the oven to 190°C/375°F/gas mark 5. Cut a cross into the top of each fig and place them standing up in a ceramic dish; pour the Amaretto or Mastika liqueur over the figs and then feed into the centre of each one a spoonful of honey.

Bake the figs for 15 minutes or until soft and deliciously gooey in the centre. Serve with a dollop of mascarpone or whipped cream on each portion; reserve some figs for the custard pots below.

HIDDEN SURPRISE CUSTARD POTS

This is an example of how one recipe suggests another: a little baked custard, with the surprise of amaretto-infused fig when your spoon scrapes the bottom of the pot.

Take little ceramic pots or ramekins and cover the base of each with a layer of Amaretto-baked fig, with some of the boozy juices. Then make up half the quantity of the orange-zested *galaktoboureko* custard on the previous page, and pour into the ramekins. Top each with a little extra orange zest and bake in a bain-marie at 190°C/375°F/gas mark 5 for about 15–20 minutes, until you have a set but still very slightly wobbly custard, and serve warm.

CHILLI CHOCOLATE CUPS

The Archduke was enchanted with the looks of the islanders.

'The Paxiots are famous for their beauty: the women are said to be the most beautiful in the Ionian islands, and among the most beautiful in Greece. The breath of the Venetians drifted over the whole of Greece – also of Paxos – and many of the loveliest faces carry Venetian names. Unfortunately one finds many of the men with bad teeth – only a few have a full set.'

They certainly still have a sweet tooth, and often demand something 'to sweeten my throat' after a good meal.

This is much thicker than chocolate mousse: it is a pot of luscious, melted chocolate truffle. Serve in Greek coffee or espresso cups, with a tiny spoon. If you cannot find chilli chocolate, you could use plain chocolate with the zest of two oranges and some orange liqueur; or a teaspoon of ground cinnamon.

MAKES 10 ESPRESSO CUPS

200 g (7 oz) best quality 70% dark chilli chocolate

6 large free-range egg yolks

100 g (3½ oz) caster (superfine) sugar

a tiny pinch of salt

200 ml (7 fl oz) double (heavy) cream

2 tablespoons dark rum

Break up the chocolate and allow it to melt gently in a double boiler or a bowl over a pan of hot water; then add the egg yolks, sugar and salt, and whisk together by hand. Keep stirring until it becomes thick and creamy – but do not allow it to boil. Then fold the double cream into the mixture, with the rum. When fully combined, pour the contents of your pan into a measuring jug with a spout, so that you can pour this neatly into individual cups without sticky spillage. Place each cup in the fridge to set for 6 hours or overnight.

MILA, MELI

I have always thought of these as milá, méli – *literally apples, honey; they are apple-studded fritters, drizzled with honey: the perfect example of honey as a star ingredient. They are Spiro's masterpiece.*

150 g (5 oz) self-raising flour

1½ green apples, peeled, cored, finely chopped

150 g (5 oz) mixed currants and sultanas

200 ml (7 fl oz) sunflower or vegetable oil

ground cinnamon

runny honey

Mix the flour slowly with spoonfuls of water until you have a very watery paste – like thin cream. Add the apples, sultanas and currants, then stir to combine. Heat the oil until it is very hot (you should get an instant sizzle when you drop in a teaspoonful of batter). Slide spoonfuls of the batter gently into the hot oil, turning them over when the underside is crisp and golden.

Remove on to kitchen paper, sprinkle with a little ground cinnamon, drizzle generously with runny honey, and consume still warm.

PAGOTA ICE CREAMS

'Makaronades,' grunts an old man, as some Italians moor in a flash yacht in the little port of Gaios. 'Macaroni eaters ...' The epithet resulted from the Italian occupation during the last war; but Italy has otherwise been a useful neighbour. The Venetians built romantic, now crumbling houses; you will come across the winged lion of St. Mark, the crest of Venice, above the door on a ruined house, overgrown with wild fig and wisteria ... Paxiots do not show that Italian passion for la bella figura *– wanting everything they do to look as beautiful as possible. But there is a rugged, rough-hewn Greek look that many come to prefer – an inherent beauty in a handful of wild flowers, propped up askew in a jam jar.*

Where Greeks and Italians are as one, is in their love of ice cream. In August, the islanders prepare for a modern Italian invasion: large families, chattering like magpies, arrive to strut through the square at night, to sample gelati. *Some of these are not Paxiot recipes, but inspired by ingredients the Paxiots have to hand, like bellinis, amaretto and mojitos.*

AMARETTO ICE CREAM

SERVES 8

200 g (7 oz) Amaretti
biscuits, crushed

1.2 litres (2 pints/5 cups)
whole milk

6 egg yolks

250 g (8 oz) caster
(superfine) sugar

500 g (1 lb) mascarpone

100 ml (3½ fl oz)
Amaretto liqueur

½ teaspoon almond
extract

Crush the biscuits in a plastic bag. Bring the milk to a boil in a pan, mixing in three quarters of the biscuits. Set aside to cool for half an hour. Whisk the egg yolks and sugar in a large heat-proof bowl over a pan of simmering water, until thick and creamy, so you can draw out a ribbon of the mixture. Then whisk in the milk and biscuit mixture and transfer it all to a saucepan. Stir over a very low heat – do not allow it to boil, or it will curdle; when it is lightly thickened, remove it from the heat and immediately stand the pan in a bowl of cold water. Lightly whisk together the mascarpone, Amaretto and almond extract in a bowl, to break down any lumps in the mascarpone, and add to the cooled mixture. Pour it into an ice cream machine and churn. To serve, sprinkle the remaining crushed biscuits over each portion.

KAIMAKI ICE CREAM

Mastika or mastic comes from the pistacia lentiscus; it is produced by tapping the trees of the resin they weep. What oozes out hardens into a brittle, which makes white crystal 'tears'. Throughout ancient history, mastic was chewed as chewing gum; our word masticate comes from it. Most of the world's mastic comes from the island of Chios, where almost half the trees were destroyed recently in catastrophic fires: an environmental and gastronomic tragedy. So mastic should be treasured. One of its most famous incarnations is the 'submarine', the ipovrihio, a thick glutinous white spoonful of sweetness, which you immerse in a glass of cold water, stirring and sucking the spoon; loved by children – and adults, nostalgic for childhood. Kaimaki ice cream has a wonderful, unusual feel in the mouth. It used to be served in one of the cafés in Loggos – then it disappeared. I was told, sadly, that no tourists ever asked for it …

SERVES 4–6

½ teaspoon mastic crystals

300 ml (10 fl oz/1¼ cups) whole milk

½ tablespoon Mastika liqueur

100 g (3½ oz) caster (superfine) sugar

3 egg yolks, beaten

300 ml (10 fl oz/1¼ cups) whipping cream

In a pestle and mortar, pulverise the mastic with a little sugar into fine powder. Combine the milk, ground mastic, liqueur and sugar in a saucepan and cook over a low heat until the sugar has dissolved and the milk is almost boiling – but do not allow it to boil. Beat the eggs in a bowl then add the hot milk in a thin stream, whisking the entire time to avoid scrambling the eggs. Do this slowly and gently. When completely combined, return the mixture to the pan and cook over a gentle heat until the mixture has thickened very slightly. You now have custard; do not allow it to scramble!

Take another bowl and beat the cream until it forms soft peaks, then combine the whipped cream with the custard, using an electric mixer to beat to a smooth mixture. Allow to cool thoroughly before churning in an ice cream machine as per the manufacturer's instructions.

ICE CREAM OF FRESH FIGS AND FIG LEAVES

Suddenly I smelt something so seductive that I had to stop in my tracks. It was a fig tree: the perfume came not from figs (for which it was too early), but from the leaves themselves … a smell of honey and pepper, hinting at sunshine. I had long wanted to capture this when I found this recipe in Caroline Liddell and Robin Weir's book on ices. The fig leaves – if you can get them – add an extra dimension; but if you just have ripe figs, it will still be a spectacular ice cream.

MAKES ABOUT 1 LITRE

450 g (15 oz) ripe figs

3 tablespoons water

3 large egg yolks

100 g (3½ oz) granulated sugar

370 ml (13 fl oz/1⅔ cups) double (heavy) cream

10 fig leaves

1 teaspoon lemon juice

Trim the stems from the figs, quarter them and place in a single layer at the base of a large pan, add the water and bring to a simmer, then cover and cook gently for about 15 minutes until the figs are perfectly tender. Allow to cool and blend briefly in a food processor, using the pulse facility, so the mixture remains chunky. Chill in a covered bowl.

Whisk the egg yolks with the sugar until they are pale and frothy. In a pan, bring the cream to just below boiling point and dribble it into the egg mixture, whisking all the while. Then place the bowl over a pan of simmering water, stirring the custard, taking care that it does not boil. When thickened sufficiently to coat the back of a spoon, plunge the base of the pan into cold water to halt the cooking process. Rinse and dry the fig leaves and submerge them into the hot custard. Allow them to infuse into the custard, covered with clingfilm, overnight in the fridge.

Strain the custard and stir in the fig pulp; add the lemon juice then freeze in the traditional manner or churn until the mixture is like softly-whipped cream. Scrape into plastic freezer boxes, cover with greaseproof paper and a lid, label and freeze. If you can, serve this fresh; if frozen, allow 20 minutes in the fridge to soften before serving.

ROSEMARY 'ICE CREAM' OF FROZEN YOGHURT

A dazzlingly white 'ice cream' made from only 2 per cent fat Greek yoghurt. Simple to make and with a delicate astringency.

SERVES 4

300 g (10 oz) caster (superfine) sugar

300 ml (10 fl oz/1¼ cups) water

handful fresh rosemary leaves

800 g (1 lb 10 oz) 2% fat Greek yoghurt

Put the sugar in a small saucepan, add the water and gently heat, stirring to dissolve, until you have a syrup. Add the rosemary leaves and crush them into the sugar syrup with a wooden spoon, to release their oils; raise the temperature so that the syrup reaches boiling point and then lower the heat, to simmer gently for 5 minutes more. Remove the pan from the heat and allow the contents to infuse in the pan for at least 4 hours or overnight.

Put the sugar syrup through a sieve over a large bowl and discard the rosemary. Add the yoghurt and stir to mix then chill. Churn in an ice cream maker according to the manufacturer's instructions. Serve in solitary splendour in little white bowls, garnished with a rosemary sprig, with little shortbread or almond biscuits; or serve with some fresh strawberries or poached fruit.

FRESH BASIL ICE CREAM

250 g (8 oz) caster sugar

1 litre (1¾ pints/4 cups) whole milk

500 ml (16 fl oz/2 cups) double (heavy) cream

100 g (3½ oz) fresh basil, including stalks

Take a large saucepan and bring all the ingredients slowly to boiling point, then simmer very gently for 3 minutes. Set the pan aside to cool; after 5 minutes, when the contents are cool enough to touch, cover the surface with clingfilm, to prevent a skin forming. Refrigerate for two hours then strain the cold contents through a muslin-lined sieve, and churn in an ice cream machine, according to the manufacturer's instructions. Serve as fresh as possible.

MOJITO SORBET OR GRANITA

A tingling, refreshing lime and mint sorbet or a granita; pour a tot of white rum over it (though children and teetotallers will be perfectly happy without).

SERVES 4

500 g (1 lb) caster (superfine) sugar

500 ml (16 fl oz/2 cups) water

zest of 4 limes

juice of 4–5 limes, yielding 170 ml (6 fl oz/¾ cup) juice

handful mint leaves

white rum to taste

Make sugar syrup by mixing the sugar and water in a saucepan, adding the lime zest and bringing it to the boil. Allow it to dissolve thoroughly, then take it off the heat and leave it until cool.

To make the sorbet, stir in the lime juice and pour the cool syrup into your ice-cream maker and churn according to the manufacturer's instructions.

To make granita, use the instructions which follow on page 219. Shortly before it is ready, very finely chop the mint, removing any stalks, and scatter it into the sorbet or granita to be churned and mixed thoroughly during the final stages. To serve, spoon out portions into bowls or glasses – and allow your guests to garnish each sorbet with a little white rum at the table. Eat immediately, as it melts quickly.

Note: I'm not usually a fan of ready-made cocktail mixes, as their flavours can seem a little harsh; but when frozen … mojito mixes work well.

BELLINI SORBET

On Paxos, sparkling Prosecco is much more common than Champagne; and peaches are everywhere – so bellinis are often the party drink of choice. This recipe comes from Caroline Liddell and Robin Weir's definitive book on ices. You can use condensed peach purée – now available in supermarkets; although this fresh fruit version is somehow more true to the peach.

SERVES 4–6

200 g (7 oz) caster (superfine) sugar

200 ml (7 fl oz) water

4 large ripe peaches

juice of 1 lemon

375 ml (13 fl oz/1⅔ cups) Prosecco

1 egg white

Make sugar syrup by heating caster sugar in the water. Place the peaches in a bowl and pour boiling water over them to cover them completely, and leave for one minute. Drain them, and as soon as they are cool enough to handle, slip off their skins. Roughly chop each fruit, removing the remains of the stalk and the stone. Put the sugar syrup in a food processor or blender, add the fruit and blend until smooth. Press the mixture through a sieve which you have placed over a bowl, then stir in the lemon juice. Cover and chill in the fridge. When your mixture is cold, stir in chilled Prosecco. Lightly beat an egg white and add this too. Churn in an ice cream machine according to the manufacturer's instructions.

TO MAKE ICE CREAM WITHOUT A MACHINE

Pour your chilled mixture into a strong plastic container with a lid – do not fill it to the top, as you will be mixing it up at intervals. Cover with the lid and put in the coldest part of your freezer. Check after 1½ hours; the mixture should have frozen to a firm ring of ice on the sides and bottom, with a slushier middle. Take out the mixture and beat for a few seconds with an electric hand mixer until you have an even slush, or, using a fork, mash it all up to a slushy consistency. As quickly as you can, return the ice to the container, cover it and put back in the freezer. This process should be repeated at least twice, hourly. After the third session of mixing, the ice cream will need to be frozen for an hour so that it is firm enough to serve. Note: if you only have a small freezer at the top of your fridge, you may want to transfer the ice cream to a deeper, smaller box when you have finished mixing it. To serve, transfer your ice cream to the main body of the fridge for about 15–20 minutes before serving.

Remember if you are including alcohol it will take longer to freeze, so it may be better to prepare a day in advance. As alcohol alters how ices freeze, you can reduce the time they are 'warmed' in the fridge before they are ready to serve.

TO MAKE A GRANITA

Pour the mixture into a shallow plastic container, with a snap-on lid, leaving room to allow you to mix, and freeze for about an hour, until the mixture has formed a rim around the edge and begun to freeze at the bottom. Using a fork, scrape away and combine everything so that you have an even mush; repeat this every 30 minutes for the next 2½ hours – or until you have a smooth consistency of ice crystals. If possible, eat granita at once; though it will keep for up to 4 hours, if you stir it once or twice to break up any clumps of ice around the edges.

Εξαιρετικός επιτραπέζιος
ξηρός ερυθρός οίνος

Το κρασί αυτό έγινε με φροντίδα και μεράκι
από διαλεκτές ποικιλίες σταφυλιών
στο αμπέλι μας στο νησί των Αντιπάξων.

12%vol   750 cc

ΠΑΡΑΓΩΓΕΙΑ-ΟΙΝΟΠΟΙΗΣΗ-ΕΜΦΙΑΛΩΣΗ: ΕΥΤΥΧΙΑ ΜΟΥΡΙΚΗ
ΑΡ. ΑΔΕΙΑΣ ΗΓΡ/22-0813/05   Πλάτανος Παξών

RED DRY TABLE WINE - GREECE

"WINE"
FROM ANTIPAXOS

CHAPTER 10
FESTIVALS, PARTIES & DRINKS

The Paxiot appetite for celebration is astonishing, when you count all the Saints' Days, Name Days, and festivals – pagan, national, Christian and Orthodox – to which they enthusiastically subject themselves. From food rituals like Cheese Sunday to the wild exultation of Easter; from front doors with wreaths of flowers on the first of May to the bombastic Ochi! Day in October, these festivals pass like amber beads on a komboloi: containing something strange and ancient, but with a reassuring familiarity; both timeless, and experienced afresh each time.

Some have Easter; others, empty mouths.
PAXIOT SAYING

JOINING THE REBELS

March 25th is one of those days into which the Greeks pack the pagan, the religious and the political. It commemorates one of the holiest days of the Greek Orthodox Church, when the archangel Gabriel announced to the Blessed Virgin that she would bear a child. And on this same day in 1821, across the water from Paxos in Patras, Bishop Germanos raised a banner in defiance of the hated Turks and their occupation. It was the beginning of the War of Independence: the Greeks rose up with a single cry – Eleftheria i Thanatos! – Freedom or Death! Their fighters were supported by leading European intellectuals of the day; in a passionate decision that was to lead to his death, Byron joined them ...

To celebrate all this, we needed dried cod. In one of the old pandopoleia – *'everything shops' – we found what we were looking for. How to convey the pell-mell glories of a* pandopoleion? *Old-fashioned tins with labels of products not seen since one's childhood are stacked crazily beside matches, dried rusks and faded tea towels; hand-bound twig brooms beside curling white paper napkins; two old men sat smoking, the flat cap of Greece welded over their heads.*

Rock hard and dry as tinder, the dried cod stank. It stank with a full, high-pitched smell, hitting the top C of fishiness. Spiro wrapped the fish in two plastic bags in the back of the van; nevertheless, fragments of the dust left a fishy smell which meant his passengers turned uneasily (Is that you?) for weeks. We deposited it with Spiro's mother, Electra, who put the dried cod in a large pot of water, with a stone from the sea to weigh it down. It was then soaked and boiled up with several changes of water, over days; the stone serving to keep the fish immersed, and thus the smell down, though Electra's home retained a perfume of cod for quite a while.

We took our prepared cod to the olive press, where Ourania had peeled potatoes and garlic, halved lemons and made the crucial ingredient, skordalia, *with an ancient white stone pestle and mortar. I have to confess that we consumed large quantities of local wine; and the magnificent cod, potato, garlic and lemon stew, ladled into vast soup bowls, went down speedily. It might be cold and raining outside; but inside the olive press, lit by an olive wood fire in the huge domed fireplace, we had tasted the Greek sun.*

SMOKED HADDOCK, LEMON, POTATO AND BAY LEAF STEW

With polite apologies to the rebels of 25th March, I have made a version of this stew more simply using un-dyed smoked haddock, with potatoes, bay leaves, pepper and saffron, finished with good olive oil, fresh lemon juice and spoonfuls of skordalia. *It is inexpensive; and it follows certain authentic principles of Greek cooking, notably the Paxiots' use of the starchy water in which the potatoes have been boiled, which magically forms the sauce of the stew.*

SERVES 4

1½ tablespoons light olive oil

2 onions, finely chopped

2 garlic cloves, finely chopped

900 g (2 lb) un-dyed smoked haddock fillets

4 medium potatoes, peeled and cut into 1 cm (½ in) thick slices

6 black peppercorns and freshly ground black pepper

pinch of saffron

3 fresh bay leaves

juice of 3 lemons

1 tablespoon extra-virgin olive oil

To serve:

freshly-made *skordalia*

extra-virgin olive oil

large handful parsley

Heat the oil in a frying pan and add the onion and garlic, sweating them on a low heat until completely soft, but not browned; set aside. Clean the pan and add the haddock fillets, cover with water, bring to the boil and simmer, covered, for 5 minutes until the fish begins to flake apart. Remove the fish, allow to cool and then strip the flesh into chunks, discarding the skin and any bones.

Wipe clean the frying pan, then add the potatoes and enough water to cover them. Add the peppercorns, saffron and bay leaves, bring to a simmer and cook the potatoes until tender and beginning to break apart; drain off the cooking water *but leave enough in the pan to just cover the potatoes* – this forms the sauce. Add half the lemon juice, the cooked onion, garlic and the fish and bring to a simmer with 1 tablespoon of extra-virgin olive oil. Grind some black pepper onto the fish and allow the ingredients to amalgamate.

Taste and add lemon juice if you wish – it should be very lemony. Warm 4 deep plates or soup bowls, and ladle portions of the stew with a generous spoonful of *skordalia* (see page 34); top with a good drizzle of extra-virgin olive oil and some freshly chopped parsley for freshness and contrast.

FEAST AND FAST

The Greek word for carnival is apokries, *from* apokreas, *'from meat', because carnival is followed by fasting, without meat. So celebrate: there will be no opportunity to indulge over the forty days of Lent. Since this festival has been topped up by the wild exhibitionism of Venetian carnival, it is rather special. People dress up – often in wild, cross-dressing costumes – and are liberated to play fools of misrule, the pagan origins of which seem very close to the surface. Clean Monday is the start of Lent; but a few Sundays before this, there is* Tyrini, *Cheese Sunday (to use up what is left of the cheese that you won't be allowed to eat during Lent); two Thursdays before that, there is* Tsiknopemti, *the Thursday of the smell of roasting lamb…*

Unlike the arid islands of the Aegean, Paxos is intensely green. It receives torrents of rain through the winter, blown across from the mountains on the mainland. A spring walk is a poignant reminder of what those with countryside parched by fertilisers and insecticides have lost. Every inch, even by the roadsides, is blanketed with wild flowers.

Spring is coming! Such house-proud cleaning, scrubbing, white-washing of steps and walls with lime! Kerbstones and corners of buildings all receive a white coating, so that in the moonlight the village seems to be dancing with ghostly, geometric brilliance. Even the dog's kennel is spruced up for springtime.

It is Good Friday and we go to pick up Spiro's mother Electra and one of the aunties. They are in their best clothes, blue eyes blazing from kind, lined faces. At the port we step into what looks like an evacuation boat: broad-bellied and beamy, a fishing boat packed with people of all ages. We slowly chug to the island of Agia Panagia – isle of the Blessed Virgin – where we climb to a tiny jewelled church, dive-bombed by screaming gulls protecting their eggs in nests among the rocks.

Within the dark of the church, candles are lit. The entire church glows – icons, carvings, faded red silk banners. The priest begins to sing through a massive frizz of white beard. On leaving the church, we form a procession, with our little candles alight, right round the walls of the convent. There is something very plain, simple and cleansing about the whole procedure; and when we get back to the boat – having collected some miniature seaweeds to whet the appetite – we all find that we are tremendously hungry.

Easter on the island is something terrific: the islanders take a whole month
to prepare for it, and as long to recover. Children have gone singing from
house to house, 'Lady of the house, give us your eggs, the chickens' nests
are full...' to collect eggs, so that they can be dyed red on Megali Pemti, *the*
Thursday before Good Friday. Round the island, food is collected, bartered,
and given with love. There are distant relatives coming home, to cater for.
Little boys run home with their arms full of the tsoureki, *brown spiced bread*
like a bosom, topped in a riot of symbolism, with a nipple of red egg ...

On Easter Saturday, the priest finds himself locked out of his own church.
The front door is barred. He goes round to the back, which is also locked. He
knocks loudly on the door, and is denied, twice. A third time, a voice from
inside the church asks 'Who goes there?' The priest shouts that it is the King
of Glory; bolts are withdrawn; he kicks open the door and bowls into the
church, the congregation in his wake. The floor has been laid with myrtle and
bay leaves; one of the poignant smells of Easter.

The service over, the front door opens and priest and people spill out,
lighting candles to give light to one another; they take them in a flickering
procession to the tiny waterfront. There is general hugging and kissing, and
cries of 'Christos Anesti!', 'Christ is Risen'; to which we reply, 'Alithos Anesti!'
– 'He is Risen indeed!'

Celebrating Easter is a national compulsion: you have got to be part of it.
Even the poorest of villages somehow have collected money for a spectacular
fireworks display. Safety is ignored; young boys (and grown men who should
know better) fire guns wildly, and set off firecrackers under foot.

On Easter Sunday, after the pandemonium and elation of the night before,
heavenly silence falls on the island. Families gather to eat, and eat, and eat.
Roast lamb or kid on a spit; there is kokoretsi, *vast salads; sweets,* tsoureki;
and young and old crack red-dyed hard-boiled eggs together, for luck. If
you're not roasting a lamb yourself, because you are in mourning, alone, or
cannot afford one, you must partake of some with others.

TO MAKE RED EGGS FOR EASTER

The red is supposed to represent the blood of Christ – and the shells the tomb, which is cracked open; so that Christ is not only Risen, but hatched. Rubber gloves are crucial here, as the dye can stain your hands. Traditionally the red dye came from boiling onion skins. You can use natural red food colouring; or you will find some supermarkets and online Greek grocery stores sell ready-to-go Anatoli egg dyeing kits.

Bring a dozen eggs – best in two batches – very slowly to the boil, so that they don't crack, and simmer them for a good six minutes; then turn off the heat and leave them in the water for 10 minutes to cool and become hard. Dissolve dye in a cup of hot water; add some olive oil, and 125 ml (4 fl oz/½ cup) of white wine vinegar. Stir in the dye, and lower in your six eggs; add enough water to immerse the eggs. Leave them for 2–3 minutes, turning them around with a spoon, so that they cover evenly. Remove them with a slotted spoon to drain on a plate lined with paper towels, and repeat with the remaining eggs. When they are completely dry – they will be dull in hue – put on your rubber gloves again, so that you can polish each egg by rubbing them gently with cotton wool or a paper towel, dipped in olive oil, for a good shine.

TSOUREKI

Easter wouldn't be Easter without this Greek spiced sweet bread. It is flavoured with two (to me, deeply romantic) Greek ingredients. Mastika *comes from the tiny dried crystals of resin from the mastic tree that grows on the island of Chios – when the trees weep their resin, they are 'bled' and these dried tears are ground to make a powder – and* mahlepi, *which is made from the ground kernels of cherry stones.*

For the yeast:

1 teaspoon sugar

60 ml (2 fl oz/¼ cup) lukewarm water

10 g (⅓ oz) fast-acting dried yeast

For the dough:

2 large eggs

90 g (3 oz) caster (superfine) sugar

50 g (2 oz) unsalted butter, melted

60 ml (2 fl oz/¼ cup) warm milk

zest of 1 orange and 1 lemon

1 teaspoon vanilla extract

½ teaspoon finely ground mastic or ½ tablespoon mastika liqueur

½ teaspoon *mahlepi*

350 g (12 oz) strong white bread flour

pinch of salt

To glaze:

1 egg yolk

1 tablespoon milk

1 red hard-boiled egg

Dissolve sugar in the water in a small bowl and sprinkle in the yeast, whisk, and leave covered to froth up for a quarter of an hour. Stir the liquid again before using it. Beat the eggs lightly in a large bowl then add the sugar a little at a time, whisking until dissolved. Add melted butter, warm milk, lemon and orange zest and vanilla extract, and mix well. Add the yeast liquid, salt, ground mastic and *mahlepi* (see Suppliers, page 263). Mix in a food processor with a bread hook at a slow speed, adding flour until the dough no longer sticks to the bowl. (If working by hand, knead for 15 minutes, with a drop of oil on your hands if they become too sticky.)

Leave the dough covered for 3 hours to rise until doubled in size. Turn onto a board, punch it down and knead it for a couple of minutes. Then leave it to rest in a covered bowl for a further two hours; knock back the dough again and roll it out roughly into a rectangle, and then into a thick sausage about a foot long. Coil in a circle in a roasting tin lined with baking parchment, pushing up the dough so that it is domed in the centre. Beat the egg and a tablespoon of milk and paint this all over the surface. Gently press a polished red hard-boiled egg to stand up in the dough and bake in a preheated oven at 200°C/400°F/gas mark 6 for 5 minutes, then lower to 180°C/350°F/gas mark 4 for about 20 minutes; remove when deep, glossy brown and firm to the touch, to cool.

CHRISTOUYENNA:
CHRISTMAS – EX-PAT FOOD

It is perhaps lucky for the islanders' constitutions that Christmas is a lesser festivity. But Paxos has a small population of British residents: a few live on the island the whole year round. They share a passionate (and to the Paxiots, often incomprehensible) devotion to their own foodstuffs. Their 'home thoughts from abroad' often take the form of yearnings for Marmite or marmalade ... once I arrived clutching a longed-for Melton Mowbray pork pie.

This culinary nostalgia is most apparent when entertaining at Christmas: ex-pats will serve turkey with all the trimmings with a loving fidelity to detail they might not bother with, if they were still at home. This has resulted in an interesting commingling of recipes.

MINCEPITA – ONE BIG MINCE PIE

Think of this as one large, cut-and-come-again Christmas mince pie. The addition of golden syrup to the pastry makes it crumbly and irresistible.

SERVES 8

250 g (8 oz) plain (all-purpose) flour

1 teaspoon baking powder (baking soda)

125 g (4 oz) butter

90 g (3 oz) golden (light corn) syrup

1 large egg yolk

250 g (8 oz) mincemeat

1 tablespoon brandy, rum or medium sherry

icing sugar to decorate

thick cream, to serve

Sift the flour and baking powder together, then rub in the butter. Blend the syrup and egg yolk together – it is supposed to be sticky, so persevere – then mix this into the dry ingredients, and work to a pastry. Grease a shallow baking tin about 18 cm (7 in) across and roll out half to fit the base. Add brandy, rum or sherry to the mincemeat, and spread the mixture over the base, then cover with the rest of the dough. Pinch the edges and prick the top all over with a fork and bake at 180°C/350°F/ gas mark 4 for about 35 minutes. Allow to cool. Sift icing sugar over the top. Serve cut into slices, with extra brandy or rum poured over, and some thick cream.

HOLE IN THE TOAD

Malcolm and Mary lived in a house they designed, looking down towards the sea. When they died, Mary's daughter, Sarah, nurtured the house. Sarah has inherited her mother's intuitive way with plants; she is also a remarkably good cook. She has cooked many more elaborate dishes; but this Yorkshire pudding, in which she used the glorious roasted vegetables left over from the Christmas turkey, instead of sausages, makes the perfect kitchen supper on Boxing night. 'It is hole in the toad!' said Spiro triumphantly. Of course it is.

SERVES 6

left-over roasted vegetables and stuffing

For the pudding:

4 large eggs

300 ml (10 fl oz/1¼ cups) milk

½ teaspoon salt

freshly ground black pepper

250 g (8 oz) plain (all-purpose) flour

3 tablespoons dripping or fat

For the roast vegetables: an ad-hoc collection to accompany turkey, cooked towards the end of its cooking time. Place in a hot oven at 200°C/400°F/gas mark 6 for about 45 minutes, turning occasionally. Potatoes first: peel then parboil them for 5 minutes in salted water; toss them in olive oil, liberally cover in sea salt and chopped fresh rosemary. Prepare vegetables like carrots, parsnips, celeriac, swede, beetroot, pumpkin and squash in bite-sized chunks. These will take about half an hour, with shallots and bulbs of garlic left unpeeled. Finally add leeks, cut into chunks. Cover all in oil and fat from your roast, season and sprinkle with thyme and rosemary.

For the pudding, heat the oven to 220°C/425°F/gas mark 7. Beat the eggs and the milk together in a large bowl with the salt and lots of freshly ground black pepper. Let this stand for 15 minutes, then whisk in the flour to make a smooth batter. Put the dripping or fat into a large roasting tin, and heat it in the oven until smokingly hot – this is crucial to success. Pour in the batter and quickly dot the surface with vegetables and stuffing. Return to the oven on a high shelf and bake for about 20–25 minutes to rise, golden and puffy.

PITAS FOR A PARTY

Greece has its own delicious street food – now, alas, dying out in the march of McDonaldisation. This is the pita: *it is a world away from those pallid pockets of plastic dough found in our supermarkets. It is also the perfect party food. You simply roll and quickly fry circles of dough to the puffy consistency of naan bread. Take little chunks of pork* souvlaki, *or crisp shards of roast lamb, add some dense, home-made tomato sauce, chopped onion, a dollop of* tzatziki *– and wrap them in the warm pita, with a greaseproof napkin, so that you can eat it on the go. If you shudder at stale doner kebabs in late-night stalls, I urge you to try this. On a summer evening with a barbecue, it would be a big hit with a party of teenagers.*

MAKES ABOUT 8–12

tomato sauce (page 257)

500 g (1 lb) strong white bread flour

10 g (⅓ oz) salt

2 teaspoons caster (super-fine) sugar

10 g (⅓ oz) fast-acting dried yeast

30 g (1 oz) unsalted butter, softened

300 ml (10 fl oz/1¼ cups) cool water

light olive oil

Make a fresh, thick tomato sauce.

In a large mixing bowl add the flour, then put the salt and sugar to one side of the bowl, and the yeast to the other. (Salt can inhibit the working of the yeast, before it has got a chance to start.) Add the butter and three quarters of the water, then mix with your fingers, dribbling in the rest of the water until you have collected all the flour together and formed a soft dough. Knead the dough on a floured surface for about 8 minutes; when smooth, put it into a lightly oiled bowl covered with clingfilm and leave in a warm place to rise until doubled in size. To cook, divide your dough into 12 pieces and roll each piece into a ball, then roll out each ball into a circle to fit snugly into your frying-pan. Heat the pan with a tablespoon of olive oil, and when it starts to smoke, place a dough circle in the pan and fry it quickly, one side for 2 minutes, the other for 1 minute. Cook the rest, adding a little more oil to the pan as needed; they will have nice brown splodges over them from contact with the pan.

Spread a layer of tomato sauce over the centre of the *pita*, scatter with crisp brown cubes of pork or lamb, a spoonful of thick *tzatziki*, some raw onion and tomato, and fold into a wrap, secure with a circle of greaseproof paper. Eat – forget elegance here – in the hand.

WATERMELON VODKAS AND DAIQUIRIS

Spiro once carved a small hole in the skin of a large watermelon and inserted the neck of a full bottle of vodka. To my astonishment, in the course of the day, the melon 'drank' the vodka. Slices of cold, vodka-sated watermelon are a very good thing indeed. Simply whizzed in a blender with some ice, it made a very refreshing drink. The daiquiri can be made with white rum.

enough watermelon to
make 250 ml (8 fl oz/1 cup)

60 ml (2 fl oz/¼ cup) Barcardi
or any white rum

15 ml (1 tablespoon) lime juice

dash of sugar syrup (optional)

Whizz chunks of watermelon from which you have extracted the seeds in a blender with a couple of ice cubes. Pour out 250 ml then add the white rum and mix. Pour into a long glass, add lime juice and a dash of sugar syrup if you wish. The Paxiots like it exuberantly garnished (silly to be shy of cliché here) with mint, and pink blooms of bougainvillea.

STRAWBERRY BELLINIS

Bellinis are very popular with the Paxiots, whose part-Italian heritage makes them thoroughly at home with Prosecco. You can whizz your strawberries speedily in a blender to make a purée, as they do in bars – but I think it's a method which defuses, rather than captures, the perfume of the strawberries, and means that you have the woodiness of the seeds in your drink. I prefer to ooze them. Once you have tried this method, you will probably never look back – and any of the left-over clear, pure strawberry juice will make glorious jellies. Increase the quantities depending on your numbers of guests, or make in batches. The following will serve about a dozen glasses. Left-over juice can be made into jellies: warm juice in a pan with softened gelatine, allow to cool and set in glasses or moulds.

Wash the strawberries but leave them whole; no need to hull them. Place them in a large ceramic bowl or pudding basin, and cover it securely with clingfilm. Place the bowl inside a deep pan, and fill the pan with water to halfway up the ceramic bowl: this is your bain-marie. Cover the pan and simmer gently for an hour. You will find that the strawberries ooze out their juice as if in the warmth of the sun. Place a large sieve over a bowl, and cover the surface of the sieve with muslin. Gently tip out the strawberry mush onto the muslin, and allow it to drip through into the bowl over a couple of hours. Press down with the back of a spoon to extract as much juice as possible.

You will find that a litre pudding basin takes 500 g (1 lb) of hulled strawberries, which should make half a litre (16 fl oz) of beautiful, clear strawberry juice. Repeat with separate batches, as you need. It can be stored sealed in sterilised bottles in the fridge for up to three days; but do not allow it to get warm, as it will ferment! Simply add to chilled Prosecco; though I must admit I like it with dry Champagne.

JASMINE MARTINI

Keep your vodka in the freezer, so that it is thick and ice-cold. You can buy jasmine tea pearls (see suppliers on page 263) – the fresher and more scented, the better – to infuse in a cup of freshly-boiled water. Allow to cool. When ready to make the martini, mix together 75 ml (2½ fl oz/⅓ cup) vodka with 30 ml (1 fl oz/2 tablespoons) of jasmine tea, add a dash of gomme syrup, to taste; add zest of lime and garnish with fresh jasmine flowers, and finely-cut lime peel.

FRESH PEAR WITH TEQUILA

If your pears are very ripe and sweet, they can be peeled, cored, and pulped in a blender. If not, take three pears, peel, halve and core them and put them in a pan with the juice and grated zest of half a lemon and 120 g (4 oz) caster (superfine) sugar. Bring to the boil and simmer until the pears are soft. Allow to cool. Put the pears into a food processor, with 2 tablespoons of the cooking syrup and blend to a thick purée. Pour 40 ml (1½ fl oz/3 tablespoons) of the purée into a martini glass and add 60 ml (2 fl oz/¼ cup) of tequila, with a dash of lime juice to taste. Serve chilled, with a salt rim on the glass.

TZINTZIBIRA
GINGER BEER

When the British took over the islands in the first half of the 19th century, they brought with them cricket – and ginger beer. It has entered the islanders' national cuisine: refreshing on a hot day; a life-saver for the hung-over. Young Phivos (Phoebus, as in Apollo) makes his own, which he sells at Bournaos' café. This stuff is best fresh, and, like all fizzy brews, you need to watch it. Fill small bottles – 200 ml (7 fl oz) is ideal – and as they are fermenting, unscrew the cap a little to release any gas. Keep these bottles somewhere cool, and in a place where any sticky explosions will do least damage …

It is an acknowledged fact that ginger beer turns out a little differently each time: if you follow this basic recipe first, you will be able to refine it to your own particular taste.

2 lemons

3 tablespoons peeled freshly grated ginger

250 g (8 oz) caster (superfine) sugar

½ teaspoon cream of tartar

3 litres (5 pints) water

1 teaspoon dried yeast

For 3 litres (5 pints) of ginger beer you need plastic bottles with caps: for economy, you can thoroughly clean and re-use small plastic cola bottles or individual-sized plastic water bottles with plastic screw caps.

Extract the juice from the lemons and the zest from one, and put this into a large preserving pan with a lid. Add the ginger, sugar, cream of tartar and 1 litre (1¾ pints) of water. Heat gently, stirring to dissolve the sugar, then simmer for 5 minutes. Allow to cool a little, then add 1½ litres (2 pints) of water and sprinkle over the yeast. Cover with a lid and leave overnight. Strain off the liquid and pour into plastic bottles, leaving a space of 5 cm (2 in) at the top to allow for the fizz. Screw the lids on tightly. Store somewhere cool – and check often; you will see a slight distortion in the plastic bottles as the pressure builds up. Unscrew the bottles to allow some of the pressure of the fermenting ginger beer to escape, to avoid explosions. Store in a cool place and serve after one or two days; do not leave in the bottle too long. Serve with ice cubes in tall glasses.

ISLAND LIMONCELLO

Yes, this island version is made with 96 per cent proof alcohol – to be used with respect and drunk with caution. A less alcoholic plain vodka can be substituted; infuse it for twice as long and omit the water.

peel of 6 unwaxed, organic lemons, pith removed

500 ml (16 fl oz/2 cups) 96% proof alcohol

caster (superfine) sugar

water

Place the lemon peel in fine strips into a Kilner or preserving jar, and cover with the alcohol. Leave, turning occasionally, somewhere cool. After a couple of days, the alcohol will have started to turn lemon colour; then dilute the mixture to thirds so that it is one part alcohol, one part sugar and one part water; you are therefore left, after fifteen days, with a drink that is for consumption in tiny shots – as it will still be 48 per cent proof.

MY LIMONCELLO

Commercially-made limoncello is extremely sweet; this is more tart, which I much prefer; or try an orange version using four navel oranges.

peel of 8 unwaxed or washed lemons

1 bottle good vodka

4 sprigs thyme (lemon thyme if you have it)

180 g (6 oz) caster (superfine) sugar

Sterilise a large Kilner or preserving jar big enough to hold a bottle of vodka. Add the lemon peel (without pith) then add the vodka. Put the sugar into a saucepan with enough water to cover it. Bring it to the boil then simmer it until completely dissolved – about 3 minutes – and leave it to cool completely. Add the sprigs of thyme to the Kilner jar and then pour over the syrup. Leave the sealed jar in a dark, cool cupboard for a month, shaking and turning it over during the first week. After a month, decant the vodka through a sieve which you have lined with muslin, into a measuring jug, so that you can easily pour the vodka into a clean bottle; (I use a plastic funnel lined with a paper coffee filter, which takes longer to drip through, but gives perfect clarity to the finished drink). Seal and store somewhere cool.

THE HERMIT'S LEMONADE

One winter I rented an old house near the Eremitis cliffs. Eremitis means hermit; this was where the hermit monk of Boikatika lived. The Archduke used to visit him in the evenings, to hear the marvellous tales of his journeys, both seafaring and spiritual. In the summer, the monk moved to lonely Antipaxos, to tend the vines. The Archduke so missed his conversation that he would sail across the strait for visits that, he said, refreshed his soul: 'His hut was so small that there was no room inside, so we sat on a stone bench in front and chatted happily together while he pressed lemons, added a little sugar out of an old tin box and presented me with lemonade …'

Here is a recipe for a simple lemonade, in tribute to two old friends whose conversation one should have loved to overhear.

For the simplest lemonade, add 100 g (3½ oz) caster sugar to the juice of 4 large lemons – or 5 smaller ones – in a large jug, add some ice, and top up with sparkling mineral water. Stir well to combine and serve immediately.

To make lemonade to store, take about 6 large lemons, which preferably should be unwaxed; if not, scrub them in warm water – otherwise just rinse them. Pare the fine zest from 3 lemons, making sure you do not include the bitter white pith, and put this into a large bowl with the squeezed juice of all 6 lemons. Add the sugar, then pour in 1½ litres (2¾ pints/6 cups) of boiling water. Stir well, cover and leave overnight in the refrigerator. Next morning, stir the liquid and taste it – adding a little more sugar if you think it needs it. Err on the side of tartness. Then strain the liquid through muslin into a bowl with a pouring spout – use this to pour the liquid through a funnel into sterilised, clean bottles, which you can cork. Serve this lemonade neat – it goes well with vodka! Or dilute it with soda water, swirl with ice – and a slice of fresh, peeled root ginger at the bottom of each glass will add a little fire amid the ice.

Best of all, pick some sprigs of fresh rosemary and immerse these in the undiluted lemonade in a large sealed container and refrigerate it, at least overnight, to infuse deliciously into the lemonade. Strain and serve over ice in tall glasses. Why should such a simple addition elevate the taste so wonderfully? It surpasses all expectations.

DEPARTURES

'Little Spiro! Little Spiro!' his grandmother would call, from her bedroom off the living room. From his parents' marriage, Spiro's grandmother had lived with them; and while he was still tiny, she was sent to the mainland to the big hospital at Ioannina, gravely ill. Lugubrious doctors did tests; pronounced it was cancer; since there was no point in operating, she was sent home. She returned to the bosom of the family, and prepared for death. Each morning she would call out to her tiny grandson, 'Spiraki! Are my papoutsia *there?' Her best slippers were indeed there, waiting to receive her feet when a corpse. 'Is the wine there?' Indeed it was – heavy flagons of the best wine, for the funeral.*

This funeral wine had to be changed several times, because in waiting patiently for Spiro's grandmother to die, it had gone sour. She flouted the gloomy diagnosis to live for another twenty-five years. As I became more at home in Paxos, I too went to funerals. I now find something distant and over-decorous in our modern urban ceremonies. Strangers officiate; sometimes the priest does not know the deceased. After the blandness of a suburban crematorium, the cheerless cups of tea and shop-bought sausage rolls ...

Much of the food associated with saying farewell in Paxos goes back to pre-Christian times. There is something profoundly moving and wholehearted about preparing food to launch the soul into the next world. I much prefer the Greek route; would you prefer to sent on your journey with fresh fish and pomegranates, or a slice of tired quiche?

SPERNA

Sperná *is an ancient dish from pre-Christian times, served at a feast in September: the fruit and the nuts celebrate harvest. It is known as* kolliva *when served at the funeral of a man 'who has lived many good days'. Whilst* sperná *is to celebrate life, it is prepared differently to celebrate the loss of a loved one:* kolliva *is decorated with almonds and silver balls spelling out religious symbols and the initials of the departed, to be blessed by the priest in a 5,000 year-old custom still followed by the Greek Orthodox Church. This is what Persephone was supposed to have eaten in Hades.*

To serve 12 plus, boil 500 g (1 lb) barley or whole wheat in water, until it has swelled to twice the size, and squeeze the liquid from it through a fine clean cloth. Boil 250 g (8 oz) almonds in a little water until the skins slip off easily, and lightly toast 125 g (4 oz) sesame seeds in a dry frying pan, taking care they don't burn. Combine 250 g (8 oz) each of walnuts, sultanas and flaked almonds, a pinch of dried aniseed, the toasted sesame seeds, 250 g (8 oz) silver aniseed balls, a bowl of fresh pomegranate seeds, and mix thoroughly with a little ouzo and icing sugar, so that it glistens like coloured jewels. Decorate a large bowl with orange leaves and roses; serve portions in tiny dishes with little spoons. Also good for breakfast; heavenly muesli for children.

LOUKOUMADES

This is a real carpe diem *recipe. Crisp and gold on the outside, they are soft within, sweet and irresistible.* Loukoumades *are fried quickly, like French* beignets; *to be made on demand, and served immediately. This is Spiro's country recipe for a small quantity with his authentic measurements – done by eye, not weight; when he says a cup, he means a filled teacup!*

SERVES 4

10 g (⅓ oz) fast-acting dried yeast

up to 220 ml (7½ fl oz) warm water

1 teaspoon sugar

250 g (8 oz) plain (all-purpose) flour

pinch of salt

20 ml (¾ fl oz) light olive oil

sunflower oil for frying

For the syrup:

½ teacup honey

1 teacup water

½ teacup caster (superfine) sugar

ground cinnamon to garnish

For chocolate sauce (optional):

100 g (3½ oz) plain (unsweetened) chocolate

2 tablespoons double (heavy) cream

Sprinkle yeast over half the lukewarm water with a teaspoon of sugar and let it stand for a quarter of an hour until you can see the yeast working, then stir it to make it smooth. Add the flour, salt and olive oil and work it until it is smooth and thick; gradually add the rest of the water to make a dough. Cover the bowl and let the mixture rise in a warm place for 2 hours, until puffed up to at least twice its original volume. Knock the dough back and repeat, allowing it to rise again.

Heat the oil in a deep-fat fryer or a deep pot to come one-third of the way up the sides, to avoid spitting. Wet your hands, take a handful of the dough, and squeeze out a small portion, no bigger than a ping-pong ball, onto a spoon. Cut off the dough and roll it against the spoon to make a ball. Lower it on a long-handled spoon into the hot oil. Fry a few at a time, using the spoon to push them under the surface to fry evenly until golden all over. Drain on kitchen paper.

Gently warm the honey with the water and sugar to dissolve into syrup. Toss in the *loukoumades* to bathe them, remove and dust them generously with cinnamon. Serve with vanilla ice cream or a swirl of chocolate sauce, made by melting dark chocolate very gently in a bowl above simmering water (to avoid it becoming granular from over-heating) with some double cream, stirred gently to form a glossy sauce.

A FAREWELL AT FONTANA

For once the beloved old dog did not come out to greet us; he merely looked up with doleful eyes. This taverna belonged to friends; in winter, when we turned up for coffee with a shot of something strengthening against the cold, there was warm, affectionate banter. Now it was silent; Eleonora, the lovely daughter, had died two weeks earlier from cancer, at only forty-three. The taverna had closed, despite the busy season, while mourning ceremonies and infinite sadness enveloped the place; then I noticed it had re-opened.

The patron Yorgo came out and – so welcome, when other restaurants boast a long menu, which cannot all be fresh – simply told us what had come from the fishing boats that morning, and he had made himself.

A plate of home-made briam: *warm, yielding vegetables in a sauce of fresh tomatoes and herbs. Each bite-sized chunk was cooked to perfection, each taste intact: gentle on the palate, comforting, good. Then the* mydia: *a steaming platter of mussels without adornment, save a few shavings of sweet steamed garlic; moist plump morsels which tasted, for once, purely of the sea. He had just let the heat open them and served them. We had eaten more than we needed, when a shy young girl came out with a final, unlooked-for dish.*

If there is a collective noun for loukoumades, *it should, perhaps, be astonishment; these little hot doughnuts crackle as one bites through the crisp, cinnamon-perfumed surface into a soft interior. They had been drizzled over with dark chocolate sauce to cut through the sweetness.*

It was a gesture that was unreservedly, triumphantly Greek. As a parting gift, it showed all the love in the house.

THE KNOWLEDGE

Much cooking know-how – like using your spoon to fold, not stir, an *avgolemono* in its final stages, to keep the froth light and airy; letting cooked potatoes cool before adding them to *skordalia*; adding drip by drip, to avoid something curdling – is what island cooks do without noticing.

TOMATOES

When you are selecting tomatoes, welcome irregularities. Tomatoes grown to be the same size have been developed with criteria other than taste in mind. Hold them in your hand: if they are weighty, it is with juice. Unless your tomatoes have been grown organically without pesticides, wash their skins; and cut out the core, which is the part of the tomato which will have stored chemical fertilizers from its feed. If you are forced to use tomatoes of little flavour, a tiny touch of chilli or a pinch of fresh cayenne, with a little pinch of sugar, may help a fresh tomato sauce.

HOME-MADE TOMATO SAUCE

To remind you of summer in the winter months: scale up the quantities when there is a glut of tomatoes. Wash and sterilise some glass preserving jars in the dishwasher, or by immersing them in a pot of boiling water for 20 minutes; lift out with tongs and allow them to dry. If, sadly, your tomatoes are not organic, wash the skins with care. Fill a large pot with about 2 kg (4½ lb) of tomatoes, which you have chopped very roughly, having removed the stalks and cores. Add a red onion, sliced, some leaves of bay, thyme and rosemary and a large pinch of salt, together with about 100 ml (3½ fl oz) of water. Heat, stirring, and when the tomatoes come to the boil, cook for 10 minutes until the contents acquire a deeper colour and are soft. You may pass the mush through a sieve for a smooth purée; or leave it chunky and rustic, as you prefer. Take off the heat and allow it to cool slightly before ladling into the jars and sealing tightly. Keep the jars in a dark, cool cupboard and consume within six months; serve liberally on pasta, in soups and in stews.

PREPARING ARTICHOKES

To trim globe artichokes, when you wish to serve them whole, take hold of the stalk and cut the tough tips from the artichoke leaves with sturdy kitchen scissors. Use a sharp chef's knife to cut off the stalk flush with the base, so that the artichoke will sit upright on its bottom. Then cut off the pointed top by cutting through the leaves. The artichoke is now ready to be cooked.

To prepare an artichoke heart, pull away or cut off all the large leaves, and cut off the stalk flush with the base, using a sharp chef's knife.

In the centre there will be a soft cone of purplish leaves; cut across these just above the choke – you will see the hairy fibres peeping through. Prepare a couple of lemons, halved, so that you can keep rubbing the exposed artichoke with lemon juice, to prevent it browning. Take a small paring knife and trim off the remaining leaves around the bottom, then take a small spoon and scoop out the hairy choke, taking care to remove all the fibres. Rub the exposed surface of the hollow generously with lemon juice; you can now cook them, or freeze them.

TO FRY LITTLE FISH

Take fresh whitebait, or *marides*, and heat some good-quality vegetable oil in a deep, heavy pan, to reach a depth of about 4 cm (1½ in). Dry the fish well on kitchen paper, and roll them in a mixture of seasoned flour and semolina so that they are well coated; if you wish, you can add a little cayenne pepper. Shake off any excess and drop them gently into the hot oil, moving them around while they fry. Scoop the fish out with a slotted spoon once they are slightly browned and crisp. Season them with sea salt and black pepper while still hot. So they stay crisp, do not squeeze lemon juice over the fish before serving; serve your guests with lemon wedges to do this.

TO GUT A MACKEREL

Place mackerel on its back and ease open the gill side flaps below its head with a knife; sever them and discard. Using scissors, or a sharp, small knife, trim off the fins, then slit open the belly of the fish and remove the guts with your fingers. Rinse the fish thoroughly, inside and out, under cold, running water, and rub the interior cavity carefully, to remove any traces of blood, as this will affect the flavour and look of the cooked fish.

TO SCALE A FISH LIKE A RED MULLET

Hold the fish by the tail. Scrape away the scales with a small sharp knife, keeping the knife blade horizontal to the fish, and working towards the head. Check with your fingers that all the scales have been removed.

FISH: SUSTAINABILITY

Nowadays, it is crucial to have the latest information on how stocks of different fish are faring, and avoid breeding seasons. The difference is the impact of the catch. Look for day boats and line-caught fish which offer sustainable fishing; your fishmonger should advise. See the Marine Stewardship Council, *www.msc.org* for advice on stocks internationally.

TO FRY A RED MULLET

Barbouni, red mullet, is widely available and it is sustainable; it is so easy to prepare and cook that it is a good place to start. Other fish can be treated similarly.

Carefully scrape off the scales, remove the gills and guts. Leave on the head, but wash the fish very well, removing any evidence of blood from the belly cavity; season it well with salt and pepper, sprinkle with the juice of a lemon, then leave the fish to marinate for 10 minutes. Put flour, seasoned with lots of salt and pepper (or a little cayenne pepper) into a plastic bag, insert the fish into the bag and shake it until the fish is well coated. Heat plenty of light olive oil until it is hot but not smoking and fry the fish; it will take about 5–7 minutes on each side, depending on the size – the outside should look well done and crisp. Serve with lemon wedges.

TO BONE A HERRING OR A SARDINE

Take a sharp knife and cut below the head, pulling the head away from the body just before you cut through and remove the guts. Then slice down the back of the fish, pulling the tip of your knife closely against one side of the backbone as you do so. Do not cut into the belly; having cut along the backbone, you can open the herring or sardine out into a fantail. Then turn the fish so you can gently cut away the backbone and remove the small bones beside it. Discard the head, guts and bones and rinse the fish thoroughly under cold, running water.

FISH ON THE BARBECUE

Clean the fish by cutting down through its belly from head to tail, then remove and discard the guts. With a sharp knife, run your knife down the body to get rid of the scales. Wash the fish thoroughly inside and out with cold water. Then dry the fish thoroughly using kitchen paper. If you have a fish grille, put your fish in this; otherwise, simply oil the bars of your barbecue, and turn the fish very gently. If you are unsure whether the fish is done, with the blade of a sharp knife make a small cut near the spine – the flesh should be white, opaque but still moist. Stir finely chopped parsley leaves and some lemon juice into a little olive oil, season plentifully and drizzle over the fish, with lemon quarters on the side. No other intervention needed.

LATHOLEMONO

This is a classic Greek oil and lemon dressing, judged by taste: use approximately 2 parts olive oil, one part freshly squeezed lemon juice, with finely chopped fresh parsley, or dill, marjoram, oregano or thyme, and salt and pepper; parsley, but no garlic – especially if served with fish or shellfish – so it does not overpower the light, fresh taste of the fish.

BIANCO: POACHING FISH

The word *bianco* shows the Paxiots' shared inheritance with the Italians: this dish is white – no tomato is allowed. Fish with delicate flesh like bream and sea bass can be poached with thyme, bay leaves, parsley, fronds of fennel and slices of onion and a little carrot, adding the juice of a lemon and some zest. The fish is immersed with the ingredients above in water, to just cover it, with a large tablespoon of olive oil and a glass of white wine added. This is brought to the boil, simmered gently until tender, seasoned and served with very lemony mayonnaise; lemon and olive oil; *avgolemono;* or *skordalia.*

HOW TO COLLECT SEA URCHINS

They are usually just under the water-line on rocks, waiting for unwary toes or fingers. Dislodge them with a sharp blow from a stick. You will find that there is a small sucker-like foot, anchoring the sea urchin to the rock. With a knife, you can cut in here to open the urchin; the five-pointed star indicates a female, with a hoard of coral eggs. Drink this delicious flesh as you would an oyster, or carefully scrape out and mix with a little olive oil as a dip for crusty bread.

TO PREPARE A LOBSTER

Kill your lobster humanely by putting it in the freezer for two hours, or put in a container and cover it with crushed ice for the same amount of time, to render it unconscious. Then, having made sure that the lobster is no longer moving, push the tip of a large, sharp, heavy knife or a skewer through the centre of the cross on its head. Once dead, you can boil it according to the recipe. When cooked, twist off the claws and legs. Crack the claws open, using the back of a knife or a small hammer.

To split a lobster in half: draw a sharp knife through the head from the shoulder up towards the eyes then put the knife down towards the tail, cutting down to the tip so that you can split the lobster completely in two. Pull the halves apart: you will see that there will be some red coral in a female; there may also be some darker roe. Reserve both as they are edible. Discard the white

gills at the top of the head and the intestinal canal which runs down the middle of the tail. The creamy green tomalley can also be taken out and reserved – it makes a fine lobster sauce.

For medallions: If you prefer not to split the lobster in half, simply turn it the right way up after you have removed the claws and legs and press down very firmly on to its back – so that you can peel off the shell from round the body, and then slice horizontally down the body into slices, known as medallions.

TO COOK A CRAYFISH

Put some smooth pebbles in the base of a large pot of water; they will retain the heat, to dispatch the crayfish as quickly as possible. Add salt and fresh dill, and bring to a very rapid boil. Put in each crayfish separately, and cook for about 5 minutes, until they turn coral red. Remove each one with tongs and when all are cooked, return them together to the pan of water and allow them to get cold in the liquid.

TO PREPARE SQUID

Take your squid in one hand, and with the other reach inside the body: you can pull the head and tentacles away. Reserve them. Now rub the mottled skin that covers the body and pull this off with your fingers. Feel inside the body for a long, hard piece of cartilage: the quill. Gently draw this out and throw it away. Wash the body inside and out under cold running water and then pull away the two side flaps from the body itself. Cut off the tentacles. If your squid still has its ink sac present, you will find it attached to the head. Remove it gently as you can use it for a wonderful sauce; then throw the remains of the head away as this part contains the entrails.

Cut the body into thick rings, slice the two side flaps into broad strips and cut the tentacles into sections. Give everything a final rinse and you are ready to cook.

TO PREPARE OCTOPUS

Cut the head below the eyes where it meets the tentacles. Turn the head inside out; remove the contents, saving the ink sac. Cut out the beak from the hole where the tentacles meet.

TO SPATCHCOCK A BIRD

Place the bird breast-side down, with the legs towards you. Using kitchen scissors or poultry shears, cut up along each side of the parson's nose and back bone to remove it, cutting through the rib bones as you go. Open the bird out and turn it over. Flatten the breast bone with the heel of your hand so that all the meat is level. To griddle, grill or barbecue the spatchcocked bird, use two skewers to secure the legs and keep the bird flat; run the skewers diagonally through the thigh into the centre of the bird. Wash hands, chopping board and equipment thoroughly after handling raw poultry.

ALMONDS

To eat green almonds straight off the tree, you can bite straight into them; though eating these green pods is an acquired taste. With teeth or a sharp stone or knife, break inside the green, suede-covered pod to find the little white centre.

These almonds are known as *tsagala* and can be added to stews, or simmered with greens. Using a small paring knife, trim around the seam of each almond, then take a large knife and embed the blade in the green casing. Carefully crack the pod down on to a chopping board; once open, pluck out the little almond and rub off the shiny film of skin which covers it. I have not seen this done in Paxos, but some people cut round the whole pod, as if they were halving a rock-hard avocado, then wash the halves, salt them and eat them whole.

A SIMPLE FISH STOCK

This can be used for cooking fish or for making a sauce. If filleting fish, or at fishmongers, keep the fish trimmings. Any white fish – haddock, cod, halibut, sea bass, bream – may be used for fish stock; lobster shells and the heads and shells of prawns and shrimp are precious. Do not use mackerel, herring or salmon as they are too strong and oily.

Wash the fish and trimmings thoroughly in cold water; cut them into pieces and put them in a saucepan with water and salt (500 g (1 lb) of fish or trimmings to 1 litre (1¾ pints) of cold water – scaled up depending on your dish. Bring slowly to a boil, skimming off any residue that rises to the surface. Add a chopped carrot and stick of celery, six sprigs of parsley, a couple of bay leaves, six white peppercorns and a couple of strips of lemon rind; do not use too many vegetables, as this will only darken the stock and blunt the fish flavour. Allow the stock to simmer slowly at a gentle bubble for up to 1½ hours.

TO CLARIFY STOCK

Bring the strained broth to the boil, whisk in two stiffly beaten egg whites and let them rise up the pan, carrying all the bits and pieces with them. Remove the pan from the heat before it boils over and don't whisk the stock after the egg whites have coagulated. Return the pan to a low heat and let the stock simmer under its raft of egg white for a good 20 minutes before straining it into a bowl through a layer of damp paper towel or, better still, a fine cloth in a wire sieve. Any well-flavoured jellied fish, meat or vegetable stock can be clarified in this way.

MOÚSTOS AND *PETIMÉZI*

Grape must, *moústos,* dribbles from grapes at the beginning of becoming wine. You crush grapes in a large wooden trough – or use a ceramic bowl with a potato masher, if you are doing this at home – then strain the contents through fine muslin, to obtain as much juice as you can. Leave it suspended to drain into the bowl for a day. In the winter, the Paxiots make *moustalevriá* by cooking the must with semolina flour until it is a thick paste, served sprinkled with nuts and sesame seeds: a very, very ancient sweet. When *moústos* is cooked, and reduced to thick syrup, it can be used as a sweetener; and this is *petimézi.* It can be used instead of aged, sweet balsamic vinegar; try sipping a teaspoon to start your day.

TO PRESERVE CAPER BERRIES

If you pick a few wild caper berries and leaves on Antipaxos, take care not to strip or damage these rare bushes. To preserve capers and some of their leaves, plunge briefly into boiling water, then immediately refresh with cold. They are then put into sterilised jars to a mixture of one third ber-ries, one third wine vinegar and one third water, then sealed. This, I think, is better than the salting method, which shrivels the berries.

TO STORE CHEESE

Free your feta! If you have bought feta in a plastic pack, liberate it when you get it home. Plastic packets of feta go hard, chalky and bad in the fridge. Store it in a lidded plastic container filled with clean water to which you add enough salt for it to taste very slightly salty.

TO PREPARE PRICKLY PEARS – WITHOUT GETTING PRICKLED!

The microscopic hairs on the prickly pear are impossible to remove once embedded in your skin or lips; they are difficult to see and cling to surfaces like chopping boards. The secret is to take a small fork and a little sharp knife, like the small blade from a Swiss army knife. Spear your prickly pear firmly with a fork then cut off the top to make a flat surface. Place this flat side on to a clean surface (a plastic chopping board is ideal). Then, using the fork to keep the fruit steady, take your knife down the fruit in vertical slices, removing the peel; finally, cut off the top. At no time should the cut surface touch an area of your chopping board which has received the skin or fine fibrous hairs: that way, you will be sure that you can slice and eat a glistening, nude prickly pear without fear of ingesting prickles. Slice it and congratulate yourself.

BIBLIOGRAPHY & SUPPLIERS

The late Patience Gray's wonderful *Honey from a Weed: Fasting and Feasting in Tuscany, Catalonia, The Cyclades and Apulia*, Prospect Books, is one of the finest food books ever written for those who want to understand the old ways. She and 'the sculptor' lived in wild places in Carrara in Tuscany; in Catalonia; and in Neolithic conditions on Naxos. She records the ancient way of life of the people, cooking without a kitchen – sometimes with only a single pot on a fire, and water to be carried from a spring. Arcane, erudite and wise, without her identification of the Greek names for fish, herbs and fungi, I would not have recognised what swam past me, or lay underfoot.

Margarita Luzzatto's wonderful translation of *Paxos and Antipaxos* by Archduke Salvator, edited by Geoffrey and Hilary Herdman and first published in 2011 by Geoffrey Herdman, (geoffrey@10dpg.com for sales), is the source of the wonderful 19th century detail in this book.

All the works of food writers Alan Davidson and Jane Grigson are recommended, especially those on seafood and on fruit and vegetables.

The following also have my heartfelt recommendation:

Barron, Rosemary, *Flavours of Greece*, Grub Street London, 2010.
Boyd, Lucy, *Kitchen Memories*, HarperCollins, 2013.
Conran, Caroline and Terence, *The Cook Book*, Mitchell Beazley, 1980.
Hoffman, Susanna, *The Olive and the Caper*, Workman, 2004.
Jacobs, Susie, *Recipes from a Greek Island*, Conran Octopus, 1991.
Karas Vianilos, Theresa, *The Complete Greek Cook Book*, Avenel, 1970.
Kiros, Tessa, *Limoncello and Linen Water*, Murdoch Books, 2012.
Kremezi, Aglaia, *The Food of the Greek Islands*, Houghton Mifflin, 2000.
Ladenis, Nico, *My Gastronomy*, Ebury Press, 1987.
Liddell, Caroline and Weir, Robin, *Ices: the definitive guide*, Grub Street, 1990.
Moudiotis, George, *Traditional Greek Cooking*, Garnet Publishing, 1998.
Tonks, Mitch, *Fish: The Complete Seafood Companion*, Pavilion Books, 2009.

SUPPLIERS

Finding suppliers of specialist ingredients has been transformed by the arrival of the internet. *greekfood.about.com* will guide you towards produce available in your region; see also *www.odysea.com* and *www.atheniangrocery.co.uk* for online sales. These have mail order delicatessens for cheeses, coffee, spices, halva, oil, pulses, wines, ouzo, mastika and mahlepi. Algaran, *www.irishseaweed.ie*, sells organic seaweed.

INDEX

green leaves 123
rustic *hortopitas* (simple weed
pies) 62–3
wild green soup 124

H
haddock
smoked haddock, lemon, potato
and bay leaf stew 224–5
haricot beans
fasoulada (simple bean soup) 66
herrings 259
citrus-marinated sardines or
herrings 96–7
horseradish
hot beetroot soufflé with
horseradish and an anchovy
sauce 88–9
horta see weeds

I
ice cream 219
amaretto ice cream 210–11
fresh basil ice cream 215
ice cream of fresh figs and fig
leaves 213
kaimaki (mastic) ice cream 212
rosemary 'ice cream' of frozen
yoghurt 214–15

J
John Dory, *christopsaro*
whole John Dory with tomatoes
and fennel 104–5

K
kebabs, *souvlakia* 143
kolliva 252–3
kolokithokeftedes (courgette
fritters) 29

L
lamb 133
lamb, mint and walnut pies
56–7

lamb salad with watermelon,
pomegranate and mint 140
lamb with artichokes 137
a little lamb terrine 148–9
Millennium night shepherd's pie
144–5
paidakia (little lamb cutlets)
138–9
pitas for a party 236–7
Spiro's meat Paxos Pie 60–1
whole roast lamb on a spit 134–5
leeks
winter casserole of tongue 146
lemons
avgolemono (lemon, egg and
chicken soup) 40–1
Greek lemon bread 184–5
the hermit's lemonade 248–9
latholemono (lemon and oil
dressing) 259
limoncello 246–7
limes
mojito sorbet or granita 216–17
limoncello 246–7
limpets, *patales* 128–9
lobster, to prepare 260
chilled soup of cantaloupe melon
with lobster 38–9
loukoumades (doughnuts) 254

M
mackerel, cleaning 258
mahlepi 231, 236
tsoureki (spiced Easter bread)
231
marides, smoked 92–3
marinades 96–7, 161
martini, jasmine 242
mastika 231
kaimaki ice cream 212
tsoureki (spiced Easter bread)
231
melons
chilled soup of cantaloupe melon
with lobster 38–9

lamb salad with watermelon,
pomegranate and mint 140
watermelon vodkas and daiquiris
238
mezedes, meze 21–47
mizythra cheese 165
bruschetta of figs, *mizythra*
cheese and green leaves 32–3
salad of *mizythra*, orange and
radicchio 77
mojito sorbet or granita 216
mousse
fresh cucumber, mint and dill
mousse 24–5
moustos (grape must) 262
mulling spices 153

N
naranje 162–3
nuts
sperna (mixed grains) 252–3

O
Octopus, to prepare 261
Odysseus' octopus 94–5
olive oil 174–5, *175*
oranges
naranje (preserved orange sweet)
162–3

P
paidakia (little lamb cutlets)
138–9
partridge with mulled pears 152–3
pasta dishes
crab in orange juice and zest with
pappardelle 112–13
sea bass with linguine and wild
mushrooms 100–1
peaches
Bellini sorbet 218
pears
fresh pear with tequila 243
partridge with mulled pears
152–3

ACKNOWLEDGEMENTS

For the people of Paxos, thanks are inadequate: I hope they will pardon me if I cannot include them all.

First of all thanks to my mentor, Spiros Anemogianis, patron of the Taxidi bar in Loggos, and his parents, Dodos and the late Electra; Lilly and Costas Andreadakis at Vassilis' taverna in Loggos; Yorgos Zenebisis at Karekladiko taverna at Fontana; Costas Bournaos and Donatella; Spiros and Ourania Zernos at Vontsas taverna; Stamatella and Mimis Apergis at Lakka; Nick and Jane Anemogianis; Ourania Dalietou for hospitality at the Olive Press Museum and for her cooking; Katerina Doui for showing me the artistry of her cheese-making; Themis Boikos; Cinzia Caselini, Adrianna Apergi, Evangelia Zernou and their friends, for so generously contributing dishes; Phivos, Philip and all at the Taxidi; Miltos Armenis, whose cooking at Vassilis' taverna at Loggos and then at the Eremetis restaurant, owned by Nikos and Martha Antioxos, provided inspiration for many dishes; Vassilis and his team at Loukas bakery in Loggos; Elias Dendias; Samantha Dasilva Day at Paxos Weddings; Faye Lychnou for her expert advice; Ben Bell for additional photographs on pages and Mimis Hadjianastasiou for his kind help.

In England, my thanks to Ian MacDonald of McMarmilloyd, Great Bedwyn, Wiltshire, source of wonderful marble; Robin Birley at 5 Hertford Street, London; and the Lobster Pot and Cobbs Farmshop, Hungerford, for fresh ingredients. I am grateful to Kostas Stavroulis for his assistance. William Norris, Pauline Byres and Tressa Lane generously helped with some dishes and photography in London, and Sally Cockcroft has been a constant support.

I wish particularly to thank Kate Pollard and Stephen King at Hardie Grant and my delightful agent, Judith Murray, for believing that there might be a book in there somewhere… Thanks on design are due to Nicky Barneby, Teresa Roviras, Susan Wightman and Michael Mitchell; initial editing was by the exceptional Jo Lamiri, with kind assistance from Kajal Mistry. The photographer Jonathan Lovekin has brought both Paxos and my own amateur dishes to life, working in the UK and in Paxos in circumstances which might have deterred a lesser man.

Willie Landels has guided me at every step, and made me laugh; and I thank Jan Matthews for his support, without which this book, and much else besides, would never have been achieved.

Writer and cook Belinda Harley began her career in publishing, working with such writers as Quentin Crewe, Hugh Johnson, Nico Ladenis and Terence and Caroline Conran. She has published two acclaimed cookbooks on Harry's Bar in London and on Annabel's, and has written extensively on artisan and organic food. When not working in London and cooking in Wiltshire, she escapes to Paxos, researching the traditional food and recipes of the island and re-creating them for modern cooks. Her memoir of the dog she rescued from Paxos was selected as one of Hatchards' Books of the Year.

Roast Lamb in the Olive Groves by Belinda Harley

First published in 2014 by Hardie Grant Books

Hardie Grant Books (UK)
Dudley House, North Suite
34–35 Southampton Street
London WC2E 7HF
www.hardiegrant.co.uk

Hardie Grant Books (Australia)
Ground Floor, Building 1
658 Church Street
Melbourne, VIC 3121
www.hardiegrant.com.au

British Library Cataloguing-in-Publication Data. A catalogue record for this book is available from the British Library.

ISBN: 978-174270-600-9

Publisher: Kate Pollard
Desk Editor: Kajal Mistry
Design: Nicky Barneby, Teresa Roviras, Susan Wightman & Michael Mitchell
Cover Illustration: Martin Haake

Photography © Johnathan Lovekin
Photography on pages 8, 126–7, 136, 141, 160, 175, 176, 179, 181, 239, 252, 255, 270 (top middle and bottom left) © Ben Bell
Photography on pages 15, 92, 172, 257, 258 © Belinda Harley

Colour Reproduction by p2d
Printed and bound in China by 1010

10 9 8 7 6 5 4 3 2 1